After Alexander

The Legacy of a Son

Jan Pryor

HEDDON PUBLISHING

First edition published in 2018 by Heddon Publishing.

Copyright © Jan Pryor, all rights reserved.

No part of this book may be reproduced, adapted, stored in a retrieval system or transmitted by any means, electronic, photocopying, or otherwise without prior permission of the author.

ISBN 978-1-9997027-4-8

Cover design by Catherine Clarke

Although the author and publisher have made every effort to ensure that the information in this book was correct at press time, the author and publisher do not assume and hereby disclaim any liability to any party for any loss, damage, or disruption caused by errors or omissions, whether such errors or omissions result from negligence, accident, or any other cause.

Some names have been changed in this book, in order to protect the identity of others.

www.heddonpublishing.com
www.facebook.com/heddonpublishing
@PublishHeddon

'Jan Pryor's memoir of the sudden death of her baby Alexander is powerfully honest and moving, with a thoughtful, even at times humorous, account of the long, slow march to acceptance that ensues.'
Mark McCrum

'An exquisitely written account of the death of a baby and the effect on the lives of those around it. And yet far more than this. Jan Pryor manages to touch every nerve in this brilliant memoir. A look at happy lives interrupted by the unbearable. I loved this book - spare and profound, sad yet optimistic, poignant yet not the slightest bit sentimental. Everyone who has lost a child - and, more importantly, those who haven't - should read this.'
Linda Burgess, Author and Memoirist

'A memoir of death, life and family living. Infant Alexander's brief life and sudden cot death. A family remembering; another child and the children growing up. All acutely observed and recorded by Alexander's mother with empathy, insight and openness, and thirty years of hindsight. Beautifully written and the most compelling and enlightening of family memoirs.'
Martin Richards. University of Cambridge

Jan Pryor was born in Blenheim, New Zealand, and has lived and worked in both New Zealand and the UK.

Jan originally qualified as a biochemist but, alongside raising her family, went on to become a teacher and researcher in the area of children and families, latterly at Victoria University in Wellington, New Zealand.

In 2003 she established the McKenzie Centre for the study of families and in 2008 became Chief Commissioner of the Families Commission in New Zealand.

After Alexander has been written from two perspectives: first and foremost, that of mother, and second as an expert in family dynamics. Jan has had two award-winning short stories published, and is working on a novel – about families.

For Alexander

A Blackbird Singing

It seems wrong that out of this bird,
Black, bold, a suggestion of dark
Places about it, there yet should come
Such rich music, as though the notes'
Ore were changed to a rare metal
At one touch of that bright bill.

You have heard it often, alone at your desk
In a green April, your mind drawn
Away from its work by sweet disturbance
Of the mild evening outside your room.

A slow singer, but loading each phrase
With history's overtones, love, joy
And grief learned by his dark tribe
In other orchards and passed on
Instinctively as they are now,
But fresh always with new tears.

RS Thomas

Prologue

It is the tenth day of April, 2014.

Early this morning I conceived a mission and I move toward it now. I am in Soho, London, in a side street off the pulsating artery of Shaftesbury Avenue. I turn left and left, until I see what I am seeking - a corner pub. It is exactly what I want. Dark, a little grubby; busy enough to sustain the reassurance of company, but not crowded.

There is a woman behind the bar. She is drying glasses with a tousled tea towel. Her breasts move gently with her hand movements; she is what once would have been called comely. She is looking out the window as if she is somewhere else, somewhere other than this gloomy house of beer. I ask her to tell me about the wine selection. There is only one kind of red, a Malbec from Argentina. She is vague about its provenance - this is a beer pub. I ask for a glass – large, please - and take it to a small grey table in a corner. Students at the next table are swapping notes, swallowing beer, exuding cheer. I'm perched on a stool. I can lean back against the embossed plaster wall. The ceilings are the colour of my wine. I am unremarkable in my place.

I am here to think about Alexander. He died thirty-three years ago, on this day, in this city. I am sitting with my wine at the exact hour that he and I were driven to London in a panic-stricken ambulance, escorted by two police cars. He was dying. I was screaming inside, my howls merging with those of the ambulance and the police cars.

Today, I am quiet. I do not weep into my Malbec as I had feared. I do not think in specifics about him, nor about that journey back in 1981. I do not imagine as I have on other days how he might have been at the age of thirty-four. The inexplicable enigma, that his death enabled the birth of his sister, does not revive to dumbfound me as it usually does on this day each year. I am conscious of being serene, of being blessed, of being lucky – of being strong. I want to stay here for a long time just being with my thoughts, just being at peace, just being anonymous.

I have come to London from New Zealand to meet my infant grandson Finlay. The juxtapositions are exquisite. It is a blackbird-spring sunny day, just as it was thirty-four years ago. Finlay is a dark-haired, pale-skinned, brown-eyed baby boy, with the fine features of so many babies in our family - just as Alexander was. Finlay's smiles divide his face horizontally and he warbles the song of a joyous two-month-old.

I know this grandbaby will not die, and I know he is not Alexander. He is, though, one of the reasons to write this story. When I hold him in my arms I hold the potential for an abundant lifetime, stretching with all its possibilities into the future.

People I have just met sometimes ask: 'How many children do you have?' I still draw breath, I still hesitate before answering. The correct answer, since the question is in the present tense, is three. To say 'three', though, is to absent Alexander from our lives, to pretend he has never existed. It is the easy answer and avoids the pause, the shadow crossing the eyes when he is acknowledged and I say he has died. It is also the cowardly answer. It is not denying his existence but it is concealing it for the sake of social comfort. It is a white lie.

'Four' is the real answer. It is the brave and difficult one. I don't 'have' Alexander but I have had him, and for me he is forever a member of the family. Naming him is a potent part of honouring him.

Alexander survives now in the memories of those who remember him. We are few. And so I am ready to write about him. I am ready to persuade memories to quicken, to examine the spaces between then and now, to explore and to comprehend the passage of time and self and understanding that has taken place in the last thirty-four years.

My marriage to his father, Jim, did not survive those years. This book, then, tells only my story. It is my experience of

Alexander's life and death, from a mother's perspective. Others in his family who knew him: Jim; his brother Simon; his sister Emily; his aunt and uncle, Barbara and Iain, may have different stories to tell.

I finish my glass of Malbec, leave the darkness of the pub, and come out into London sunshine. I know I'm all right, more than all right. I am strong; stronger than I would be if he had not lived and died.

One

Friday 10th April was another blackbird-spring day in our village of Bygrave in Hertfordshire. It was a week before Easter and the sun's warmth was becoming palpable, moving on from being the enticing promise it had been in March. It was the sort of day that dissolves the remnants of winter and presages the lightness of summer. It reminded me that my life was blessed, that the future was filled with the light promised by a completed family.

Simon and Emily had gone out of the door, school bags jiggling on their backs, and caught their bus to school. The novelty of catching a bus in England rather than walking to school in New Zealand was still alive for them. My sister Vellyn arrived from Buckinghamshire with her baby daughter Rebecca, to spend the day with us. Vellyn and I had time to sit with our babies and have sister-to-sister chats about the two compelling topics for mothers of infants: breastfeeding and sleep. Alexander was typical of all my babies. He slept erratically during the day and his infant brain was just beginning to perceive the possibility that night was the time to sleep for longer than two hours at a time.

After Alexander

The sun was heating the stones on the back wall of the house, so that warm waves of air bounced back into the yard. The blossoms were exhausted and were being replaced by green leaves, translucent in their infancy. Daffodils were waving their last. Lilac was blooming. Its smell took me back to childhood days, warm in my grandparents' garden, watching my grandmother hang washing onto a line propped up by a piece of wood, her body bending to lift the weight of sheets still soggy with water. Her lilac bush had leaned over my child-body, competing with the smell of soap from the laundry.

In Bygrave, it was an English spring rendered more acute by its contrast with winter. At lunchtime, Jim loped in the door, free from patients for an hour. We carried platters of cheese and wholemeal bread, salad and olives, glasses of elderflower cordial, and had lunch outside. Like lizards, we sat soaking the sun through our winter-bleached skin.

Alexander was with us, propped in his baby bouncer, and for the first time in his nearly-four-month life he tasted yoghurt. Jim spooned it into his mouth, catching drips of pink overflow on the sides of his lips. Alexander grimaced, looked startled as the first taste of something that was not breast milk assailed his tongue, then swallowed and opened his mouth for more. A few mouthfuls later, his eyelids started to lower over his eyes and he rubbed them with his fist – a sign that all mothers know means a baby is ready for a nap. I picked him up and took him upstairs. The timing was perfect – he was ready to sleep and getting the moment right meant that he would sleep for at least half an hour.

It was cooler inside, between the stone walls of the house, than it was in the garden. I wrapped Alexander in the softness of the shawl my mother had knitted for my brothers and sister and me as babies, and put him down on his sheepskin rug. His wriggle was baby-sensuous as he drifted into sleep. I kissed the back of his head.

Jim left us in the garden and drove back to Letchworth for an afternoon surgery. Vellyn put Rebecca into her carrycot to sleep and we lingered outside, chatting about our family at home in New Zealand. Quietness draped around us in the warmth. Desultory words floated between us. With Alexander's unpredictable sleeping habits, I knew the peace would be brief.

He was sleeping longer than usual, this lively little boy. I wanted to stay, to dawdle in the garden with Vellyn while he was still quiet. But a sliver of worry was starting to distract me from the sweetness of the moment. Why, though, should I worry? He was tired, his sleeping times were unpredictable, and he was simply having a longer nap than usual. I should relax.

I let another ten minutes pass and went up the stairs. He was wriggling, as babies do, in that borderland between sleep and wake, sun lighting his hair.

Vellyn and I had decided to take our children and Muffin the household spaniel out into the fields behind the house. We were going to wait until the school bus delivered Simon and

Emily home. Time, then, to make their peanut butter sandwiches while Alexander was still quiet in his bed. I went back downstairs.

Baby Rebecca woke up and Vellyn fed her. I made stacks of white-bread sandwiches with tawny fillings, and filled two drink bottles that were still functioning after being bought at Disney World a year before. Simon and Emily bounded in through the front door. 'We're going for a walk up through the fields,' I told them. 'We're just waiting for Alexander to wake up.' Muffin the mad spaniel heard the 'walk' word. Her ears separated themselves from the side of her head and she started bouncing around the kitchen.

Simon and Emily ate their sandwiches. No noise from upstairs. Alexander had obviously gone back to sleep. I'm a deep respecter of sleep for myself and everyone else. Time, though, was passing. Soon, coolness would begin to seep into the fields, and walking would be less fun. I decided to go up and see whether he was waking.

The stairs curled up to where the top step was almost opposite Alexander's bedroom door. I walked on the sides of the stairs so that they would not creak. I crept into his room.

He was pale. He was still; too still. He was not breathing. My brain froze, my legs sagged. My body refused to move. I screamed down to Vellyn.

She ran up the stairs and snatched him from his bed. Breathed into his mouth with the cool skill of a trained nurse. His chest moved with her breath, and then rose and fell without her help. He was breathing. He stayed asleep. But it was deeper than sleep. He was unconscious.

Vellyn carried his stilled body down to the front door. I could see the tiny breathing movements of his chest. He was alive but something was terribly wrong. We needed to get him to hospital. Simon and Emily hovered around the action, fear flaring in their eyes as the grown-ups panicked. I phoned Jim at the surgery. He abandoned his patients and started driving toward the village to meet us in his small old car.

The Volkswagen camping van was outside the front door; our only transport. I pulled its sliding side-door open and Vellyn, Simon and Emily clambered in. Rebecca was in her carrycot on the floor. I passed Alexander in, and Vellyn cradled my motionless baby. I drove, pushing the box-shaped vehicle around bends at speeds it was not built to go, until we met Jim driving towards us in the old sedan. I jammed the van to a halt in the middle of the road, slid the side-door open, and grasped Alexander. Jim, usually loquacious, was wordless as I told him what had happened. He focused on driving the old car at speeds it had achieved only in its youth, toward nearby Stevenage Hospital. I held our silent baby on my knee in the passenger seat. Vellyn took over the Volkswagen and drove Simon, Emily and Rebecca back to Bygrave.

At the Accident and Emergency department, a house surgeon snatched Alexander from us and wrapped him in foil, like a fish to be baked. His temperature was spiking up and down; hot then cold with no in-between. The staff moved around the nearly-empty room like insects under an upturned log, and shouted for another doctor. Someone, more senior and more composed than the house surgeon, took our silver-wrapped son away to do a lumbar puncture. 'Wait here,' he called over his shoulder as he and Alexander disappeared through grey folding doors. I wanted, more than I'd wanted anything, to follow them. I needed to be with my baby.

Jim and I sat in the quiet of the emptied A&E clinic, silent. Questions repeated themselves inside my head - *What has happened? Why?*

Please fix him.

My whole being was focused on the need to hold him, protect him and save him, yet he was through there somewhere, out of sight, out of reach. He was with others; professionals: people who knew what they were doing, who might just protect and save him for us.

A nurse came through the swinging doors into the room. Her face was neutral, revealing no emotion. 'Come with me.' Her voice was calm. Why was she not panicking too? We followed her into a small windowless room to wait – this was not, apparently, going to be a quick procedure. She left us in black plastic chairs and came back with a brown medicine bottle.

'Brandy,' she said. We gulped it, clutched each other's hands, and waited. We couldn't talk – we could find nothing to say that could be put into words. I imagined my baby being unwrapped like a parcel, his slender spine penetrated by a fat needle.

The senior doctor came into the room, this time trailing panic. 'We don't know what is wrong,' he said. 'We are going to transfer your baby to Great Ormond Street Hospital in London.' There was the greatest urgency. And no, we couldn't see him now. There was no time for that. He would be transported to London in an ambulance and I could go with him. Jim would follow in the car.

It was Friday, 5.00pm The tiny, bulky bundle that was Alexander wrapped once more in silver was loaded into the ambulance together with a registrar anaesthetist, there to watch over him on the trip to London. I climbed up the high step into the ambulance and sat in a seat that resembled a metal camp chair, in the rear. My head was touching the roof. We were encased in a dim box lit by small side windows. Alexander was in a cot strapped to a bed, the anaesthetist crouched beside him.

The stocky white vehicle pulled out of the hospital grounds. The windows of the ambulance were tinted so that outsiders could not see in, but that insiders could see out. We were driving down the familiar road from the hospital toward the junction with the A1. I could see our car in line behind us. Jim's face was blanched, his hands tight on the steering wheel. I waved. He couldn't see me.

After Alexander

Two police cars had joined the ambulance as we came to the outskirts of the town, one leading the way and one following behind, forming a red-and-blue flashing procession. As we came closer to the A1, the ambulance driver turned on flashing lights and started the siren. From my seat at the back of the vehicle it was like being backstage as a spectacle played out in front of house. The entourage turned south onto the A1, joining the thousands of other vehicles creeping toward London on a Friday afternoon, in multiple lines, like braids of a New Zealand river moving to the sea. The police cars wailed their demands to be let through the thickening ropes of traffic and the ambulance howled its need to hurry. A bizarre trio for sirens ensued as we pushed our way toward London. Jim followed the shrieking parade in the old sedan, weaving and taking the slightest of gaps between other vehicles to keep the ambulance and its escorts in sight.

Inside in his cot, Alexander looked like a diminutive space traveller; face composed, immobile. Too immobile; the anaesthetist pushed an oxygen mask over his face, leaned forward to the driver and shouted at her to go faster.

I was flooding with the primeval instinct to protect and rescue my baby. It eschewed rationality, it railed against my helplessness, trampled through reason, rendered me molten. But my unsheathed she-bear claws were impotent. They were being thwarted by the interventions of those who, my front brain knew, were better placed to help Alexander. Helplessness folded into terror, time lost its coherence. Strapped in that stainless-steel chair, all I could do was to will my baby to hold on to his diminishing life.

I needed this anaesthetist to be calm; to be competent; to keep my baby alive; to make him move and open his eyes, and cry. Instead, the silent baby invoked a contagious panic in the man, who lashed the driver to go faster. She could not go faster. It was Friday night on the A1 going south to London. She was doing what she could, a looming island of calm in the flood of the disarray behind her, in the back of her vehicle.

The ambulance left the A1, wove with its screaming retinue through suburban streets of north London and into the centre. We moved at the same pace as on the motorway, creeping around traffic, blasting through red lights, slow, slower. As we reached Great Ormond Street Hospital the police cars dropped away like fighter planes abandoning a chase and the ambulance reversed into the murky tunnel at the side of the hospital where emergencies were ejected into its care.

For a moment there was an enveloping silence, the sirens quieted and the engine of the ambulance mute. The old sedan swerved in off the street, Jim pulling the steering wheel around. His face was a pallid disc floating in the space behind the windscreen. Somehow, he had managed to stay with the ambulance through the chaos of the drive from Stevenage.

Seconds later, the back door of the ambulance was flung open and bedlam resumed as Alexander was rushed into the maw of the hospital. The flimsy husk of control I had managed to sustain on the trip shattered. I wailed, I keened, louder than the sirens had done. The ambulance driver was a robust woman. She pinned me in her arms until my screams subsided. A fierce, loving hold – she had dealt with this primitive terror before. Jim and I gripped each other's hands, and followed Alexander into the hospital.

When we found him, he was lying on bleached sheets in a cot in the intensive care unit. His body lay silent; a muted shade of medical white, unadorned in the fug of hospital heating. From the door of the room, all we could see was the black arc of his hair, his baby shape blurring into the sheets. A machine was breathing for him, inflating his lungs, counting the breaths, infusing his blood with oxygen. Around the island of his silence, a disharmony of machines was pumping, measuring, assessing, counting. They clicked, pounded and whirred their busy-ness in a macabre symphonic white noise.

He was insubstantial, pale, and so beautiful – my heart ululated inside my chest. My breasts swelled, ached in synchrony with my heart's howling. They wept milk. I pumped it into bottles, put them in the fridge for him for when he woke up. The expressing machine sucked my love, my desperation, my runnels of fear, and stored them efficiently in glass.

A parade of specialists started to appear. A cardiologist slipped softly in through the door of Alexander's room, white coat unstained by his day's work. He introduced himself. We nodded. Speech felt beyond us. He put his stethoscope on to Alexander's chest. His movements were tender, careful.

'I can't find any problems with his heart.' His voice was quiet, cautious.

A physician came in. His fingers probed Alexander's abdomen, they stroked his head. He read the black-and-red lines issuing from the machines; messages of life and death. The lines on his brow became deeper, turned into small chasms. His eyebrows formed verandas above his eyes, hiding any messages they might have held. He glanced at us, nodded, and left the room. No words, certainly no syllables of hope.

We searched the faces of every doctor who came to examine Alexander, combing them for signals of reassurance. They looked away when they saw the pleading in our eyes. No answer was the best they could do.

Every ten minutes, a nurse slid through the door, checked the tubes and drips and machines, asked if we needed anything, left again. There was only one thing we needed and we were ready to wait. We were, after all, in the best hospital in the world.

Whenever exhaustion became too strong to fight, we left our mute son in his white room and went to some beds at the end of the ward, reserved for parents of ill children. Sleep eluded us – we lay flat just long enough to gather strength for the next vigil. Other mothers and fathers told us over cups of hospital tea about their children in the ward who had come back from frightening brinks, started to breathe on their own, and woken up. We grasped their words, their optimism, and the hope they held out to us.

We sat with our baby, waiting for his miracle.

One of the machines beside him was there to register the messages of his brain but his brain was not communicating. The track of its dispatches on the river of paper had no hills or valleys; it ran in parallel with the baseline of the chart, unremittingly straight. The machine whistled; listened for the signals from his small cranium; heard nothing.

I called my mother in New Zealand; she who had pronounced Alexander extra to requirements when she knew I was pregnant with a third child.

'Mum? I'm in the hospital with Alexander.'

'Are you? What's wrong with you?'

'It's him, Mum. He's sick, really sick. He's in a coma.'

'He'll be all right, dear.'

'Mum, he might not. He might die.'

'Nonsense. No grandson of mine dies.'

I hung up.

In my head I began to offer up contracts with God, the being in whom I did not believe. As additional insurance, I offered supplications to the Juju, to Gaia, to any divinity or force I could think of who might listen to my pleas. *Save him,* the contracts said, *and I will be your disciple. Forever.*

The machines pumped his lungs, measured his temperature, searched his blood for clues. They peered into his heart, his liver, his brain, and his bones. The paper monsters churned out the latest news on his brain. There were no messages.

The line stayed flat.

I rearranged my future. I knew by now that when he awoke he would not be the baby who came into this hospital. We could adjust to that. A handicapped child could be immensely rewarding, I told myself. We would adapt our lives to encompass him and his requirements. He just needed now to wake up.

It was Sunday night. We three had been there for forty-eight hours. We can keep him alive with our machines, the doctors said, but we can't bring him back. Would you like us to keep your baby as a vegetable that you can visit every week? We don't think we should, but it's your decision. You must decide whether we can turn off the machines. Go for a walk, they said. Think about it. Walk around the block a few times, go to the park around the corner, take your time.

We walked. It was a cool spring night, the trees in the local park breathing quietly. Our son could not do that, by himself. He would never be able to.

Would you like to hold him, they asked, as we take out the tubes?

Last chance for Allah, Jehovah, Yahweh, Beelzebub, Tane. Alexander lay in his parents' arms, pure white baby, while I made my final desperate offers. There were no takers.

It was nearly Easter. He didn't wake.

I called the Queen Charlotte Hospital and cancelled the appointment to have a tubal ligation the next day.

Two

The smell of Heathrow in November 1980 was excitement mixed with anxiety. I try now to imagine our little procession through the eyes of a small person – a person as small as Emily, aged four; or Simon, aged six - making its way from the arrival gates. Bodies pressed closer, more urgently, than they did in New Zealand. Bodies with exotic voices and unfamiliar skin, some wearing flamboyant flows of colour, others sombre in grey and brown and black. Sounds of the world – incomprehensible words from the blare of loud speakers, shouts from men in dowdy uniforms, words in unfamiliar languages, flowing above their heads. Buzz and hurry and crush engulfed our little group.

The children held fast to us or to the bags and suitcases attached to us. Their father, Jim, was easy to see, his auburn hair high above most other men's heads. Their mother – me - moved like a small ocean liner with thirty-five weeks of pregnancy determining pace and deportment. My unborn baby preceded the rest of my body.

I was exulting in this pregnancy. I had been required to sign papers before we flew out of New Zealand, promising that I was not more than thirty-five weeks pregnant and that I would not "emit foul odours". I had signed happily, assuring airline officials that this pregnancy did not involve a colostomy bag.

We moved, a cautious parade, beyond the baggage carousels and through immigration booths, and spilled out under the exit sign onto the footpath outside. The London daylight was diluted, soft with haze. Eight eyes glazed with travel narrowed in its glow.

A car slid along the kerb, slowed and grew arms, as Jim's sister Barbara and her husband Iain waved, calling through open windows. Barbara, too, was pregnant. Toddler Anna opened her blue eyes wide and stared as her New Zealand cousins drooped on the footpath. In its small blue carapace this car held our soulmates and saviours-in-waiting.

With seven autonomous bodies and two in utero on board, Iain piloted the car through the labyrinth of the airport roads and drove north into Hertfordshire on the A1. In 1980 this was already an unbroken weave of cars moving north and south, from and to London. Alongside, the fields were quiet, sleeping off the excesses of summer. Trees were skeletal, crouching in the cold. An hour up the line, Iain turned east off the A1 and drove through Baldock, the little market town that was to be the centre for all our day-to-day needs for the coming year. Butcher, dentist, grocery store, stationery shop, dry cleaner – all in one modest main street.

We were finding our way to Bygrave; formally an old village and parish but actually a mere lane. We reached it by turning left out of Baldock, driving under the railway bridge, and looping right onto what felt like a one-way road through fields. A couple of miles along this curving byway, an even smaller lane turned off to the right. This was Wedon Way; an unassuming, dead-end sliver of road that was the main and only street of Bygrave. Houses straggled along each side of the road, comfortable with themselves; family homes with back gardens strewn with vegetable patches and trampolines. Our home for the next year was one of these dwellings: a two-storeyed, low-ceilinged house, with a gravel drive the shape of a smile. The family who usually lived there was in our house in New Zealand for the coming year; we had exchanged homes, dogs, cats, and medical practices. They had taken up residence in our rangy house in Christchurch and were caring for our ageing boxer. We were moving into their house in Hertfordshire and managing their capricious spaniel, Muffin.

At the end of the road was a manor house. The fields behind the single-file rows of houses on the lane were owned by the family living in this looming grey mini-castle. Pheasants, foxes, rabbits and mice lived in the crops that have been nurtured there for centuries. A public path permeated the pastures, meandering from Wedon Way up to a churchyard above the village.

Simon and Emily tumbled over the front doorstep of our new home, swarmed like puppies in and out of rooms and up and down stairs. The windowsills were low and wide, the windowpanes criss-crossed into small squares that cast exotic frames for the foliage outside. We were used to wide, high, untrammelled views from New Zealand windows – these subtle glimpses from English windows were enchanting.

Bygrave was quintessential commuter-belt England. Fathers drove or caught the train from Baldock to London for work; mothers stayed at home, cared for children until they were old enough to go to school, and met in each other's sitting rooms for coffee in the mornings. Hedges were trimmed and lawns were mowed. Families looked after each other, children roamed unsupervised and safe in the lane after school. The village played its part in raising the young.

The house we were in enfolded us, protected us from the gloom outside. The eyebrows of the windows were low, the rooms relying on internal light rather than the paltry winter offering from the sky outside. The fireplace was the core of the house while central heating around the walls of the rooms supplemented its last-century efforts. Simon and Emily found the books and toys belonging to the children who were now in New Zealand and discovering theirs. They bounced on chairs and claimed their beds in the bedroom upstairs.

Lights were on, Jim had met the challenge of turning on the central heating, and the sun was setting - it was 4.00pm. There was a scrabble at the front door, followed by a knock. Jim wrestled with the ancient latch and then turned the contemporary key below. He stood back as the door flew open with the impact of a russet missile that hurled itself through into the hall. Muffin, the resident spaniel, was home. She was ours for the rest of the year. The neighbour who delivered her into our custody emanated relief, introduced herself, issued an indeterminate invitation for dinner sometime, and left.

In the kitchen, Jim marked 'E' and 'S' on alternate days on the calendar to counter breakfast-time bickering about whose turn it was to push down the plunger in the coffee pot.

Three

Anyone observing us a few years earlier, in Christchurch in 1978, would have seen a demographically average family. Heterosexual married parents with two children exactly two years apart in age: boy first, girl second. Attractive, happy children, observers would have concluded. We, their besotted parents, regarded them as beautiful – Simon, with auburn hair that he regretted daily when he reached high school; Emily, whose eyes were green-brown pools. They bickered with and loved each other. In photos from that time, one or other has an arm around the shoulder of their sibling.

We lived in a two-storeyed, slightly worn, big-boned house, nestled in trees that kept us cool in summer and cold in winter. In the Sixties and Seventies in New Zealand, insulation was regarded as unnecessary; a sign of suspect self-indulgence. Houses like ours had, at best, an open fire and some electric heaters. Behind the house was a cracked and functional swimming pool.

Christchurch is regarded as the most English of New Zealand cities. The River Avon traipses through its core; the civic buildings are sober stone, reminiscent of those in many older English towns. In recent years, two tumultuous earthquakes have turned its gracious heart into hillocks of rubble; in 1978, such destruction was unimaginable. In those years it was imbued with serenity and restraint.

We lived in Fendalton, a suburb with a network of streets inhabited by families living in houses with rooms that opened their wide arms to hold their people, and surrounded by generous gardens planted with English trees. Jim was a General Practitioner in a practice in a nearby area of the city where the trees were smaller and the houses more narrow.

My day-to-day life in Christchurch was not typical, though, of that of a suburban housewife. Other wives in Fendalton were serene in their gardens, greeting children coming home from school and husbands at the end of their absorbing days in the office or courtroom or surgery. Cake tins were filled and dinners prepared.

I, meanwhile, was completing my Masters degree. My garden was wild and my cake tins empty. In the mornings, Jim swallowed his coffee standing up, tied his tie, and drove to tend to his daily stream of patients. Simon climbed on to his big-boy tricycle and rode down the footpath to meet his friend Dougie, who had a serious scooter. Side by side, they steered their respective transportations to school.

I made peanut butter sandwiches for Emily and pushed them into a box, with a banana. She and I clambered into the old black Rover 90, sliding over the cracked leather seats that smelled of disappeared privilege. She sat on the armrest beside me as I navigated us to the university crèche. As we came to corners, I flipped the indicator button on the wheel and an orange flag leapt out from the side of the car, telling people we were about to turn. At the age of three, Emily was a senior at the crèche. She ran in to assume her position, waving vaguely back at me.

A small but significant aspect of my daily pilgrimage to the university was a flight from the encouragement to play tennis and bridge. Disinclination, lack of the required coordination, and an allergy to card games condemned me to failing at these activities; I had few attributes to be a fitting wife for a doctor. Jim knew this when we married and he was comfortable with my lack of sporting ability, and my hungriness for academic pursuits. I fluttered at the edges of learning while he used his considerable skills to heal and reassure his patients.

It was, though, a fainthearted rebellion on my part against the persuasions of being a wife of a professional man. At most, I emanated a mild pink hue through the area in which we dwelled; a faint reflection of the impact of being in an academic world for some of my days. With Jim, I enjoyed our green suburb and our beloved children.

I belonged to a curious cohort of women in New Zealand. We occupied a position on a cusp between the traditional expectations as wives and mothers laid on those a few years our senior, and the aspirations of women just five years younger, on whom feminism was beginning to have an impact. Women of my age and older, especially those like me, growing up in areas outside the cities, were not expected to have aspirations above a defined and modest level. Nursing, teaching or working in a bank were suitable ambitions for bright young women, with the expectation that marriage would claim us in our early twenties. To go to university was to challenge those assumptions, particularly in a small town like the one in which I grew up. It was almost unknown for a young woman to contemplate a professional course such as medicine or law; it was more than enough to leave home and go to university.

Women half a decade younger than me were shedding those constrictions. We who left school in the mid-Sixties had one foot in each half of the decade. One mini-culture told us that finding a professional husband was an acceptable motivation for going to university (and preferably we should choose one with a law and a medical faculty); it was not *feminine* to aspire to be more than pliant and stylish wives.

The emerging ethos being embraced by our slightly younger sisters told us with increasing confidence that we too could have a profession, make a contribution, lead a kind of life that was accessible not just to men. Like many other early baby boomers, I felt as if I was doing the splits. Being a good wife by itself was not enough – I'd had a glimpse of the possibility of something beyond, alongside, that. On the other hand, I was not sufficiently brave to be single-minded about a professional career even if I had known what that might be. I had an itchy brain and no focus.

At high school I had been good at science. *Being good* was relative to my female (in particular) schoolmates who were not interested in the secrets of biology and physics. I was the girly swot, despite my lack of absorption in the subjects, perhaps because I was so unco-ordinated and unsporting that I was able to make up for miserable sporting prowess with nerdy achievement. At my small-town school there was little exposure to the arts, law, literature, or history. It meant that I had no knowledge of where those subjects might lead, in terms of either personal expansion or professional opportunity. There was nothing for it but science so, with no enthusiasm, in my first year at university I studied zoology, botany, mathematics and physics.

Despite a half-hearted approach to these subjects and my burgeoning interest in extracurricular activities, I was awarded an A-pass in Zoology. Embarrassment followed surprise, and was joined by confusion, when the Professor of Zoology summoned me to his office and invited me to join the honours stream. This meant taking extra laboratory classes, and being fast-tracked to a postgraduate degree. Undoubtedly there were, even in 1965, a small number of young women who could appreciate the attractions of pursuing a career looking down a microscope at tiny animals, or examining the behaviour of big ones out in a field.

I am ashamed now; not that I could not see a future for myself in any of these fields but rather I am dismayed by my perception then that the prospect of being identified as clever was to invite social suicide. Not only did small-town New Zealand offer me no models of successful, or even professional, women but it demonstrated mild disapproval. A female doctor who had joined a general practice in my town was treated with some suspicion by locals, including my parents. Somehow she wasn't quite a real doctor.

And I understood that a man would not be attracted to a nerdy woman. The spectre of a future being single, successful, and probably odd, hovered. A friend had had the same invitation from the Botany Department at the university; a part of each of us was tempted. Together, we constructed an arrangement where we could cover for each other as we did the extra laboratory classes in the honours streams. No-one, we thought, would find out.

Fear of being different won. We were too timid. Instead, we both moved to another university and took courses in microbiology and biochemistry. As subjects they were even less beguiling than dissecting the alimentary canal of a dogfish; an activity we undertook in first-year zoology laboratories. My grades in the second and third years at the second university were barely above passing.

There I met and married a *good* husband. I loved him not because he was a doctor but because he was a lovable man. He loved the part of me that was not compliant, alongside the larger portion that was. We were, though, in a social setting in Christchurch in 1978 that raised its eyebrows when I decided to go back to university to pursue subjects that roused my passion, rather than indulge in those feminine hobbies that filled in time. My study was part-time but nonetheless, to my fellow wives in the suburb, it was puzzling. 'Who irons your husband's shirts?' asked one confused wife. I did, although not at all well. Fortunately, Jim's jackets covered the creases.

It was the mystery of how children grow and learn and become the magical beings they are that fed my curiosity. That, and the burgeoning desire to exercise what I had concluded was a mediocre brain – a C-pass in stage three biochemistry was evidence of that. I started with one paper, called Developmental Psychology, with 599 other students. Simon, one year old, became a part of the university crèche a few hours a week. He was not pleased when I left him there but as soon as I'd waved too many times in farewell and disappeared, he forgot that he was abandoned and joined in whatever was happening.

I topped that first class. I was astounded, and encouraged. The desire to be a graduate student appeared, and began to grow. Perhaps my brain was not as mundane as I thought. It was a puzzling aspiration, as hard to capture as a dream in the morning. The first desire of that strength that I remember experiencing was when I was nine years old. I was passionate about horses, and that engendered a passion to have one. At twenty-seven years old, the craving to explore the limits of my brain was a surprise.

More papers followed, I took a short-cut to graduate level, and started a thesis focusing on how children understand fairy tales. By this time I had embraced Philosophy of Science; the theories of Piaget and Bronfenbrenner and Bowlby. It was heady stuff, and deeply fulfilling. Somehow, I managed to nurture our family life alongside all the excitement, and Emily was born in these years.

Being a mature student gave me an adequate balance between my divided inclinations, so that our family life was calm and sufficiently normal. The friends we made were lawyers' and other doctors' families, as well as some of my academic colleagues. I straddled two pools of political persuasion without my mind or heart doing the splits. And I was not the only fainthearted suburban revolutionary. Jenny, a friend, and the wife of a busy man, joined me in subtle rebellion against the pressure to be content with our lives of privilege. Together, we petitioned the school board to let our daughters wear culottes so they could turn somersaults or climb the jungle gym without losing their modesty. It was the first whiff of feminist ambition in our green and pleasant suburb. We did not succeed.

Four

In the decades leading up to the 1970s, families in New Zealand acquired baches. The term arose as a diminution of 'bachelor', since they originated as huts lived in by lone males, often in isolated places, in the colonisation days of New Zealand history. In the early 1970s, ownership or access to a bach was strikingly egalitarian. Rural and seaside land was cheap, and a bach was often just one room or a shed. Families of all means were able to own, or have the use of, one. More recently, the word has morphed to refer to holiday dwellings more generally and, in some cases, to alarmingly elaborate weekend mansions.

In Christchurch, we had access to two baches, one from each of our families. Jim's parents owned one that had recent origins as a small house in Wanaka, a lakeside town in the kind of landscape that inspires international moviemakers and artists. The house gazed out over a lake that lay resting in the arms of spectacular mountain ranges. On many Friday nights, Jim finished his surgery early. At home in the afternoon I sat Simon and Emily at the red kitchen table and fed them

Spaghetti Bolognese, or sausages and carrot sticks. With the back seats of our Austin Maxi folded down, sleeping bags made a children's bed that was considerably less comfortable and far more exciting than the ones in their bedroom. The boxer dog, Yaffe, stretched out with them in the back as we drove four-and-a-half hours to Wanaka uninterrupted by "are we nearly there?" from the back seat. Sleeping dog and children were easily transferred to beds in the bach. On Saturday mornings, Jim and I slept while his parents indulged their grandchildren with time and treats.

On other weekends, a similar packing routine had us driving north to my family's bach, at Anakiwa in the Marlborough Sounds, at the north end of the South Island of New Zealand. The Sounds are a region of New Zealand formed aeons ago by river valleys that sank, letting the ocean in to create arms of blue-green sea which meet native forest cascading down the sides of the hills to the edge of the water. It is a real bach; one that started as a shed and grew haphazardly to accommodate spare stainless steel cutlery, unneeded furniture, unloved art prints, a cuckoo clock, a paint-by-numbers scene I did as a child, my mother's childhood copy of *Anne of Green Gables*, Reader's Digest compilations of animals of the world, unread thrillers, a Bible and a Collins American Dictionary. It had beds for five adults. Children slept on camp stretchers and sofas.

The bach in 1954 was a section of land with a small shed on it. No water supply, no electricity, just songbirds and seabirds, an outlook over the sea in the Sound, and tranquillity. For my brother and sister and me, it was an adventure – we camped in the shed on camping beds, carried water from the creek in the bush behind, and my mother cooked on a small gas stove. Toilets were also in the bush, along a path cut by my father's mower. There we could hide with discretion behind a substantial tree, and take a trowel if it was needed for disposal.

My father set about constructing a liveable dwelling for us, paying homage to my mother's limited tolerance for living rough. All able bodies, including those of children, carried bags of gravel up through the trees in the gully behind, where the fathers from the three baches being built at the bottom had taken cement. A concrete wall was built to interrupt the flow of water in the creek coming down from the top of the hill, and from that dam they laid pipes to the dwellings below. Drinking the creek water was like drinking chilled sunlight.

My father, who had never learned formal skills of building, plumbing, or electric wiring, arranged for power to be connected. He plumbed and wired the house, his pear-shaped body leaning into his tasks, a cigarette in his mouth. A cross between a hum and a whistle escaped though the unoccupied parts of his lips. The elastic of his underpants showed as his shorts slipped a little with his exertions.

'Janny,' he'd say, 'come and hold this for me, will you? I just need to drill a hole here.' I was ecstatic.

As soon as the bach was liveable, he turned his energies to boats. He built a handsome dinghy dubbed "Queen Elizabeth". He built a launch in the shed which had been moved on to the back of the land behind the home we lived in. He made sure all of us were able by the age of ten to drive the launch and bring it safely into the wharf. He died before he was able to pass his passions onto his grandchildren; before any of them were born.

Jim and I would arrive late on a Friday night. There, at the bach, my mother reigned. Although she did not live there, she was always with us when we were there. When my father had bought the land, he had clamped haphazard additions on to the shed: a bathroom straight off the kitchen (illegal, ignored by authorities, and unchanged); a bedroom and a bunkroom, and - in 1963 - a paved deck that today has dips and hollows in its surface as the ground subsides. Through floor-to-ceiling windows is a panorama of an arm of the sea – sometimes stormy, more often smoothed to a serene blueness and studded with gannets and shags and dolphins. Beyond the water is native forest, climbing up the hill on the other side of the bay.

My mother's grandmothering vision did not extend to letting us sleep while she entertained our children. She cooked meals to an exact schedule. At 11.55am each day, she would produce a bottle of sherry and three glasses – one for her, and one each for Jim and me. Just one drink each – she was not a tippler - and lunch was nearly ready. By noon, she and we would have sipped our sherry, and it was time to eat.

'Janny, the children are *quite* good at sitting up, aren't they?'

'Janny, do you think Simon and Emily should say 'please' and 'thank you' a little more often?'

She rarely addressed Jim directly. She held him in awe shaded with resentment – a kind of inverted snobbery mixed with envy. Her exposure to professional men had always been just that – professional - and she was deferential. Now she had one in her family. The fact that I had married a doctor, she found difficult, despite Jim's gentleness with, and affection for, her. A part of him admired her awkward honesty; she took almost nothing at face value, and was unafraid to say, uncensored, what she felt. And she was my mother; he was respectful of that.

She had found me vexing as a child and when I became an adult it was a different kind of challenge. Essentially, my husband and children had interrupted her right to make demands on me. She tried – she could not help herself. And her jibes still pricked at my confidence. Often, her attacks were indirect.

'Simon and Emily, you know that psychologists aren't to be trusted, don't you? Your mother has just finished her Ph.D in Psychology, though I don't suppose she's a *real* psychologist – she works in a university.'

She wanted to love us, and no doubt she did love us in her own understanding of that feeling. Her affection was most readily expressed by bestowing material goods, often inappropriate or unambiguously dreadful. We learned to accept them with grace, and remembered to have them on show when she visited.

She had had her own particular cohort struggles. She was a bright young woman with no chance at all of furthering her education beyond the legal requirement of her age to stay at school. She was enmeshed in the complications of the Second World War, when the best and most she could do was to become a Red Cross nurse. The war ensured that as she moved into her late twenties the pool of young men to marry was diminishing. She married my father, a divorced man of forty-six, and settled into a provincial town existence where being married to a divorcee held a pervasive stigma. Her response was to put up defences and to work with my father in defiance of small-town expectations of wives. She carved out a justification and reluctant respect in the community for her abilities as a woman running a successful real estate and financial advisory business. She was eccentric, although as a child I saw that as simply being embarrassing.

She was hard to love. Her anxieties prevented her from genuine expression of her affection, so that it was delivered with distortions. It was hard for her children and grandchildren to avoid receiving it as manipulation. And at times there was no doubt – it *was* manipulation.

For example, when her youngest child, my brother, left home and went to the United States, her distress at his leaving took the form of blackmail.

'If you don't come back in the next year,' she told him, 'I'll have to sell the bach.'

She knew that it was the place he loved above all others in the world. He didn't come back the next year, and she didn't sell it – it was rescued from dispatch by the rest of the family gathering around to hold it.

Her other daughter, my sister, had not been lucky in her relationships. But now, she brought her new husband home from England. My mother's greetings were limpid. On the first morning with her, my tremulous sister and her beloved sat at breakfast with her.

'What is wrong with David?' she asked, looking at Vellyn. 'He isn't eating his bacon rind.'

Not surprisingly, they went back to England to live. A few years later, after gruelling sessions of fertility treatment, Vellyn became pregnant. My mother was staying with her in England, being feted as the guest of honour for the three months she was there. When the news came of Vellyn's pregnancy, our mother Sylvia's response was to pout and sulk; the focus of attention was no longer on her and her needs.

As adults, we learned to survive, to stave off her attacks, to feel pity for her. We realised that over-riding and underpinning her love and her wounding behaviour was her need to protect her hurt self, to shore up the walls that staved off potential threats. I once wrote a poem about her, in an attempt to understand her behaviour.

She had always been small
in body.
But from that carapace there extended volleys,
barbs, tentacles and, occasionally
loving arms.

She moved about the world with care
and suspicion
looking for attacks which sometimes
came, but more often were imagined.
Nonetheless she fired, just in case.

It was lonely inside, but safe.
We outsiders tapped for attention,
for understanding, for love.
And sometimes it came. But
mostly the taps seemed like attacks and
were shot down.

* * *

Between mealtimes at the Anakiwa bach, Simon and Emily learned to row the old aluminium dinghy left by my father in the boatshed. They dropped fishing lines over the end of the jetty, catching inedible little fish, which we cooked in the microwave and admired on our plates.

The smell of the native forest around two sides of the house was musk; sudden rush of honeyed native blossoms; scat of possums; dankness of beetles; syrupy odour of beech sap. It infused the children's memories, and mine, as adults; it continues to jolt us back to the unreflective innocence of childhoods when we go there now.

Jim and I had no reason not to take this blessed lifestyle for granted.

Five

In 1979 we had spent four months of the southern hemisphere winter in Miami. A group of New Zealand general practitioners had put together a scholarship for doctors to work in a medical centre in South Dade; a suburb to the south of the city. We had not won first prize; we were there in June, July and August, when Miami locals flee north for the cool of a northern American summer. Those who could not afford to move, and innocents like us, endured 100-degree temperatures and 90% humidity.

We had accommodation in an apartment block that was defiantly that – a block. No frills, a concrete edifice four storeys tall, with six apartments on each level. No balconies, no courtyards, but a shared swimming pool in the middle of the complex. Our apartment was on the ground floor. When we arrived, we opened its door to a stuffy, square room furnished with American chain-store furniture. We spotted the air conditioner switch on the wall and turned it on. Its setting was the norm for locals - twenty-five degrees lower than the temperature outside. We shivered, and turned it up. Lizards rested, vertical, on the walls – iridescent green and brown reptiles that entranced Simon and Emily. They stayed undisturbed, exotic inside companions.

In an apartment along the hall lived a pet-shop owner. He wandered past our door daily, with a parrot on his shoulder chatting into his ear. Sometimes he carried a baby alligator. Pets were welcome in this block.

So, too, were mixed-race marriages, in contrast to in the upmarket, gated communities nearby. It took time, coming from New Zealand, to understand that this was somewhat exceptional. In our block, African-American men gathered during the day in the sun in the car park, rapping and laughing. They didn't know it but I felt safe in that car park only when they were there. There had been a murder a few weeks earlier – a white man shot a white man.

Children, too, were allowed in this block. A single mother in another apartment had a son who played around the pool with Simon and Emily, and who came to our apartment intrigued by our pronunciation of his language. One morning, a gummy dog at a local playground nipped this tough little boy. He stared at the indentation on his leg; his skin was intact. 'I'll sue you for this,' he said to the dog's owner. He was nine.

In the apartment above us lived Barry and Susie. Barry was black, six-foot-eight tall, and as gentle as a man of that stature could be. He manoeuvred his body through space with the care of someone who had since adolescence bumped their head on door frames made for smaller-sized people. Susie was short, blonde and jiggly. Her teenage daughter, with identical blonde hair, lived with them. She offered to babysit Simon and Emily one evening and we were happy to accept. Unmitigated exposure to even our adored children was tiring and this was a chance to have a meal without their chatter.

We climbed the concrete butt-strewn staircase up to their apartment, Emily clutching her favourite book. Its title was *Alexander and his Horrible Terrible No Good Very Bad Day*. The words rolled mellifluously around her three-year-old tongue as she chanted them to Barry. She looked like a child's doll on his massive lap. His whole being was captivated. In the weeks after her recital that evening, he would rumble up to her daily by the pool, stoop down, and in his *basso profundo* voice and southern accent shout, 'Hey, Emmie, tell us the name of youuur booook!' It was some years before she recovered her equilibrium in the presence of large and loud people.

* * *

We had returned home from Miami to New Zealand via London. We wanted to make plans with Vellyn and David, and Barbara and Iain, for our coming year when we would be living nearby them in England.

On that visit to England in 1979, I also wanted to visit Martin Richards, the Director of the Medical Psychology Unit in Cambridge, which later became a Family Research Centre. He was the author of a text we had used in the postgraduate paper in Developmental Psychology at Canterbury University. My

Masters degree was not finished; nonetheless, my mature student status gave me the boldness to ask if he might employ me as a research assistant the following year while we were in the UK. To my surprise, he invited me to visit him in his office in Cambridge.

Deciding what to wear to try to impress a Cambridge don was a test. My imagination failed me, trying to guess what such a person would be like. Doctor's-wife attire felt wrong and in fact not many of my clothes were in that category. Jeans and a jersey might have been too casual – I wanted to impress him with my erudition *and* style. And what would a Cambridge don be wearing? Grey trousers and some sort of jacket, I assumed; perhaps a tie, neat and not garish. I chose a dress that I hoped defied categorisation – mildly patterned, belted at the waist, knee-length, not too formal and not too relaxed. As we drove to Cambridge, my stomach danced around inside me, churned by excitement and apprehension. I badly wanted to work with him, and I could not let myself hope too much that he might agree to let me in to what I saw as the hallowed space of a research centre in Cambridge, focusing on children's development.

Martin was dressed in black corduroy jeans, cuffs meeting socks and ageing shoes. He wore a blue shirt, crumpled and buttoned over a t-shirt. Clearly no-one ironed his shirts for him. His hair was dark, swept from deep on one side of his head across to the other, adjoining a beard that had set its own idiosyncratic boundaries. He limped across his study to greet me, circumventing stacks of books on the floor. His limp was the legacy of a car accident in which both his legs had been broken; one of them had stayed permanently shorter than the other. He had a soft voice and a lightly worn authority.

We discussed potential projects I might do in the year. We agreed to stay in touch and that I would develop a proposal that I could carry out while we were in England in 1981. I left his office excited and incredulous. Cambridge had seemed impossibly exotic and unattainable from New Zealand, and now I had the chance to be a modest part of its activities. I am sure that Martin did not notice my all-purpose dress, nor the fact that I was entranced by his gentleness and eccentricity.

* * *

Our family at that time was symmetrical – one child for each adult. Our car was designed for four passengers and their appendages, and a dog. We had the prospect of a year in the UK with Simon and Emily at school, Jim in an amiable medical centre, me immersing gently in the exotic world of Cambridge, and with time to spend with our siblings and siblings-in-law.

Why would we sabotage the tidiness of our family structure? I am still not sure. Two felt just a little too orderly, a little too neat, a little too perfect. A boy first, a girl second, exactly two years apart. With astonishing irrationality, we decided to break the symmetry that felt not quite right, and have a third baby. Once the decision was made, we knew it was the right choice for us.

It was not easy to write the letter to Martin Richards to tell him of my pregnancy. I expected, if anything, a polite sorry-and-good-luck-with-your-baby response.

'What a creative approach to child development,' he wrote back. 'When you are here, why don't you come to our weekly seminars and bring your baby with you?'

'Why,' my mother demanded of bank-tellers and shopkeepers in the small town where she lived, 'does Janny want to have another child? She has two perfectly good ones.'

* * *

In June 1980, still in a wintry Christchurch, I settled into the chair in my office in the Education Faculty at Canterbury University. I was a tutor; a role that entitled me to a cupboard with a desk and chair, and a window looking down to a path between buildings. I had inhabited it joyously; my own small but real academic space. I put books on the shelves, a pot plant on the desk, and a picture of Simon and Emily on the window sill.

Until then, no-one in the department knew that I was pregnant. One Tuesday morning, a teacher and colleague; a Philosopher of Science who had emerged from priesthood to the secular halls of academe, came into my room. I slammed shut the drawer of my desk, crumbs cascading onto the floor. I was combatting morning sickness with a flow of crackers.

'Good God, Jan, you're not pregnant are you?' His face told me he was joking.

'Yes.'

He backed out into the corridor, then edged back in again to congratulate me. I offered him a cracker. From then on, everyone in the department knew. And that made me even more a not-so-ordinary graduate student. I was not just old; I was pregnant.

Later, at the beginning of November, I was in an examination room at the university, sitting a paper in educational psychology. Invigilators paced across the front of the room, dressed in grey trousers or skirts, and sensible shirts or blouses. They flashed glances and mouthed signals to each other, scanning the room for the merest hint of doubtful behaviour. These worthy retirees were paid very little to watch over potential cheats and to carry out the official duties required for university examinations. Fellow students, young and apparently free of self-doubt, wrote vigorously, chewed the ends of pens, gazed at the walls, and wrote again, asking for extra booklets to write their answers. How could they have so much to say? My baby churned and danced under the desk in front of me; a distraction from recalling the theoretical frameworks for understanding how seven-year-olds comprehend their worlds. I didn't ask for another booklet.

The next evening, friends and neighbours gathered to meet the family with whom we were exchanging houses, cars, and dogs.

Children dodged around the legs of the adults. I rescued savouries from burning in the oven, made sure everyone had a glass of wine, and told the English family what our old boxer Yaffe liked to eat.

Three days later, we left for London. We left behind Jim's parents, who were to join us in the northern spring, and my mother, who had planned a trip for the English summer. They would all meet their new grandbaby in its first few months.

* * *

Now in England, I had a year to exult in motherhood unimpeded by study and doctor's-wife duties.

Soon after we moved into Wedon Way and warmed the house, an aerogramme arrived; a frail blue tissue that contained news from my life left behind in Christchurch. It was from my thesis supervisor. It told me that I had been awarded first-class honours for my Masters degree. It was unbelievable news, hard to comprehend, and felt unrelated to England and late pregnancy. My focus had moved to mothering and settling in a new country. That blue tissue was a fragile link to the extraordinary year just finished, of study, parenting, pregnancy and travel.

Six

Of course it is the coming, or rather the not-coming – of the baby that is beginning to dominate my thoughts a little. With less than two weeks to go, I find myself hoping that it will be early, although that's silly as it's bound to be late! The head is already engaged I think – sometimes it feels as if it's all going to fall through. Letter to my mother, December 1980

I was booked into Queen Charlotte Hospital in south-west London to have this baby. The drive from Bygrave to London on the A1 could take forty-five minutes or it could take two hours. We knew that a third baby might come with little warning. So when New Zealand friends who lived in Ealing near the hospital suggested we move into their house while they went home for Christmas, we accepted. A week before the date the baby was due, we drove into the street lined with trees bare for their winter respite, and parked in front of the Ealing house. We unloaded suitcases, children, and Muffin the spaniel. Jim pushed the front door open and we stumbled one after the other into a dark hallway. Muffin dashed in between our legs, following the scent of a recently resident cat. The lights illuminated high studded ceilings and embossed wallpaper, dark painted furniture lurking in corners of the rooms. Simon and Emily homed in on the toys left behind by the children who lived there, settling in like the adaptable rolling stones they were becoming.

We relaxed into the embrace of the dark-walled house, made gloomier by the low-hanging winter sky. In London in December, light seeps in at eight o'clock in the morning and leaks from the air by four o'clock in the afternoon. Inside was warm against the cold of the street, light against the darkness of the sky.

London was Christmas - festive as London does so well in midwinter. Dark mornings and darker evenings heightened the excitement as the four of us explored the light shows of Oxford Street and stared at magical displays in shop windows, where elves sang and princesses danced. Father Christmas greeted the children in Selfridges, sat them on his amorphous lap, and fed them lollies. Emily was cautious – he was a boomingly large man. The Snow White grotto was a cave inhabited by dwarfs, stalagmites and stalactites twinkling to the music of triangles and flutes. It was a Christmas for childhood, the Christmas we saw on Christmas cards and read about in English books during the summery festive seasons in New Zealand. It made sense in a way that hot beaches and sand between the toes did not at home.

We were light and happy. We held hands, pretended to be the Beatles crossing Abbey Road; we sang songs together and made two lists of names for the baby. We didn't know, we did not want to know, whether it was a boy or a girl.

* * *

At 7.00am on 20th December, the Christmas tree glimmered in the dark of the Ealing sitting room, pinpoints of light in its real pine tree branches. We had left it on all night so that it greeted us in the mornings, reminding us it was Christmas. Jim went downstairs to the kitchen, gave Simon and Emily a drink, and carried cups of tea up to the bedroom. I sat up and felt a damp patch on the sheet beneath me.

No panic. It was a small patch. The four of us had breakfast around the wooden kitchen table, Simon and Emily bickering again over whose turn it was to push down the coffee plunger. We had forgotten to bring the calendar from Bygrave, the one that dictated who had the privilege on 20th December. They chose their clothes for the day, and we all went to Queen Charlotte Hospital Outpatients' Department.

'It's just for a check-up, then we'll go to a pub for lunch,' we promised the children.

House surgeons, especially those in outpatients departments, take leaks seriously – more seriously than Jim and I did. I was transformed from a free-ranging person into a captive patient in the time it took to snap the plastic hospital bracelet around my wrist. I was to be induced; my baby was to be persuaded out by pharmaceutical means, for its own sake.

We called Barbara and Iain and told them that Simon and Emily were coming to stay earlier than planned. As Jim took them out of the outpatients department door, they looked back over their shoulders at their confined mother. I waved and two small hands fluttered back. They forgot about their pub lunch.

The birthing unit hummed in several keys. Silver and antiseptic, clean and spare, the latest technology was at our disposal. And the staff members were persuasive in their insistence that I should have all the benefits of modern medicine. It is not easy to consider alternatives, to ask for other options, when one's body is connected to a machine that is intent on hastening your labour and has no interest in your opinions. Efficiency was the zeitgeist of the unit.

'We are just going to put a scalp clip on your baby's head, Mrs Watt.'

Why do people shout at you when you are in a compromised position? And what *was* a scalp clip? Whatever it was, it was clamped to the baby's head to monitor its heartbeat – far more sensitive, I was assured, than an old-fashioned belt around the waist. Capable hands pushed it upward and stapled it in place on my unborn infant's skull. Having fingernails pulled would have been less painful than it was having it attached.

Jim returned. Machines were in action around the nearly-three of us. One sang the rhythm of the baby's heart, *badoom, badoom, badoom.* It was a reassuring cadence. That scalp clip was not missing a beat. Another appliance pumped oxytocin into my arm, ensuring that my sleepy uterus received the message: push this baby out. A band around my abdomen reported on me if I was not working sufficiently hard. It told the oxytocin machine to speed up, to send higher doses of the drug into my body.

It was my third labour; I was practised at dealing with the pain of contractions by now. I had learned a kind of self-hypnosis in my first pregnancy from an excitable National Childbirth Trust midwife who suggested I think of a song with many verses, sufficiently challenging that I had to think hard to remember the next one[1]. That way, I would focus on singing rather than the painful activities of a contraction. It worked. I had chosen "There's a hole in my bucket dear Eliza..." – it seemed apt. And so I sang, for this baby.

We worked together, my body and me, until I saw the baby's head between my legs. There was a pause, long enough to give me a chance to greet it. There was my baby's face, disembodied, genderless, eyelids squeezed together. It was a moment, a chance to greet our child; not yet a son and not yet a daughter.

The rest of the purple-pink body slithered out, and there was Alexander, unmistakably a boy. The name was at the top of our

---

[1] Simon had been born in London in 1974.

boy list - because we liked it, not because of Emily's book. It fitted him instantly. Perfectly, utterly, intact.

I had done enough work. I lay back and let besottedness flood in.

Like the machines, the nurses were working in overdrive in this delivery suite; several other women were at various stages of giving birth and needing attention. In this space, Jim was just another excited father, not a doctor who had delivered hundreds of other people's babies. And no-one told the oxytocin machine that my work was done. The band around my sagging middle registered no contractions, so the machine wound itself up into action, exhorting my body to resume its work. None of the distracted professional staff noticed. Jim transformed himself from besotted father to obstetrician, and turned it off at the wall.

* * *

Simon Rowley is a man who emanates calm. He is a New Zealand paediatrician who was working at Queen Charlotte and on duty that day. His hands moved over my baby with care, keeping him calm, caressing him, feeling for the slightest imperfection. It is a subtle skill, reassuring for both neonates and their mothers. He declared Alexander flawless.

Five years later, when Simon Rowley had returned home to New Zealand, we conferred a singular status on him – the only other person apart from us in the country who had met Alexander.

Our own Simon, and Emily, stepped softly into the room where Alexander and I were settled, on the post-natal ward. Their eyes were like those of cats when they come in from the dark. They touched and stroked their brother.

'Can I hold him, Mummy?' Emily's voice was quiet, her face emanating awe and delight. Her arms wrapped awkwardly around the sleeping baby. She rocked him, and passed him to Simon. Alexander did several rounds of his siblings and his father, until it was time for the three of them to go back to the house to sleep. I fell into a slumber imbued with exhaustion, achievement, and bliss.

Early the next morning they were back, watching me eat cornflakes and canned peaches from a thick bowl on a plastic tray. Jim had in his hands two cups of proper coffee, and in his pocket an oblong white envelope that was addressed to me. This unmistakeably official missive held news from that other realm of my life, the one left on the tarmac when we flew from New Zealand. It was a letter telling me that I had been awarded a Post Graduate Scholarship to do a Ph.D at Canterbury University.

I had a beloved husband, I had a baby more beautiful than any other in the world, I had two happy children, and now I had academic honours. It felt as if my life was overflowing with benedictions, with almost too much grace.

Two days later, Alexander and I went back to the big, dark house and joined the rest of the family around the Christmas tree. I propped him on the sofa in the middle of us. We were five now, and we listened to the Festival of Carols and Lessons from King's College in Cambridge. Joy to the World.

The number five is not four. It sits above four's prim symmetry. Five is not six; it sits below six's proper rows of three. It is an odd number, with a vigour that three lacks, and a cohesion that is absent in seven.

There are five virtues.

We have five basic senses and five basic tastes.

The world has five oceans.

Animals including humans have five fingers or toes on each limb.

Five is music: the perfect fifth is the space used for tuning.

The music staff has five lines.

Beethoven wrote five complete piano concertos.

Five felt true, five felt right.

* * *

We returned to Bygrave after Christmas. The days after I had come out of hospital, I was supposed to be visited by a midwife but somehow we missed her more often than not. I wrote a letter to my mother:

He is now twelve days old and seems as if he has been with us forever. Simon and Emily both do a lot with him – carry him, change him, chat to him... he really is a dear little boy, with Emily's colouring but very much Simon's features.

Bygrave had known us for just a week as a family of four. Now we were as we were meant to be – a quintet. Alexander became the centre, the focus of an adoring foursome. We were a web around him, loving and protecting.

Seven

A new year had begun. We nestled into the Bygrave house in gloomiest January, the sun appearing as a milky disc for a few hours each day. We were all adapting to a different rhythm of life. Jim drove in the mornings to the medical centre in Letchworth, a town ten minutes from our rural lane. And each morning the school bus, windows fogged with the breaths of small bodies, crept down Wedon Way, collecting children wrapped against the winter, schoolbags filled with books and extra clothes and lunches. The bus was exotic for Simon and Emily, whose privileged lives meant they had been driven in cars rather than taken on buses. Simon was smitten with buses. As a three-year-old he had begged me to be a bus driver rather than study at university. And a few days after Emily was born, he had come up with an inventive idea: 'Why don't you put her on a bus, Mummy? The bus driver will look after her.'

An easy routine settled on us. Alexander and I had six hours together each day, interspersed with lunch with Jim when he was able to come home from the surgery. Those hours with my baby were freedom to luxuriate in being a mother, free from the distractions of toddlers and the demands of studying for exams. And the vagaries of infant sleeping or not, feeding too often or not enough, of elusive burps and nappies with mysterious contents were not new, were not challenges. I had done all that before.

Village mothers encompassed us, their hospitality loosened by knowing that we were not permanent residents. I could be embraced without the scrutiny that someone moving in permanently would require. My New Zealand accent with its flat vowels rendered me unable to be pigeonholed into any particular English class so not only was I unthreatening, I was also an object of curiosity. And I could accept invitations to morning coffee, or not. Social obligations had been left behind in Christchurch.

I was one of a lane of full-time mothers of children, staying home while our husbands went to work each day. At the beginning of the road was Sarah, whose girls caught the bus each morning with Simon and Emily, and whose baby was the same age as Alexander. We had just enough in common to get together once a week, discussing motherhood and pretending not to compare our babies.

The village and nearby Baldock were a mix of working-class and middle-class families. Like chameleons, Simon and Emily adopted forms of English pronunciation that would ensure they fitted in as fast as possible. Emily's words took on a strange middle-class hue; she told me one day that her shoe lace was 'brokern'. Simon assumed the consonants, or lack of them, of his best friend, who came from a working-class family. His pronunciation was akin to that of the boy who told the teacher his name was 'Pa'erson, wiv two Ts.'

Some days I snuggled Alexander into a front pack, wrapped his head in a woollen hat, and set off along the path leading to the church. Mad Muffin yanked on her end of the lead, yapping, the scents of animals suffusing her nostrils. I let her off as we came to fallow fields hunkered down for winter rest and restoration. She dashed in a zig-zag path, following invisible trails, yelping her excitement, ignoring my pleas for her to come back. Once she ran back to me, a flapping pheasant clamped in her mouth, her whole body wagging with doggy pride at catching it. These pheasants had been moved up toward the woods near the Manor House by 'beaters', ready for the shoot planned on the weekend by the Squire. I had a plan – I would say she was not mine if anyone from the Manor House saw her. This was devious - a claim true in fact, if not in the present reality. My integrity was not tested; no-one appeared when her jaws were full of feathers.

The sun glimmered, a milky disc peering through clouds hovering at the edges of the horizon. I sang to Alexander, meandered up the hill, and wandered around the church. Ancient gravestones mouldered on disappeared graves, names erased by moss and lichen and time. We ambled back down the hill to the warmth of the house in time to greet Simon and Emily as they bounced off the bus. They needed peanut butter sandwiches and a drink before they started their current favourite activity – entertaining Alexander.

* * *

I had not entirely abandoned academia. Martin Richards' invitation to attend seminars was enticing me north to Cambridge. On Tuesday mornings Alexander and I, and Jim if he was off duty, drove the fifty minutes north from Bygrave to Cambridge. The car wove through B and C roads, between hedgerows, past stone houses and thatched roofs. Alexander, strapped into his baby seat, sang his songs, and blackbirds called their late winter tunes from the trees. Fields flowed past the car, closing in behind us, the sweetness of early rape blossom and clover infusing our journey.

In Cambridge I carried Alexander in his sling along stone-paved lanes between colleges and churches, through the market place and down Free School Lane. In a small garden outside the Old Cavendish building there was a bay tree, reaching up to the windows of the building.

If Jim had come, he and Alexander would wander around the buildings of Cambridge, exploring the lanes and gardens of the city while I sat in a seminar room alight with the seduction of the research being presented. If Jim was on duty I climbed the curling, slanted stone stairs, with Alexander in a front pack, to the seminar room on the third floor. Alexander was greeted and clasped by the miscellany of people who were there to listen to lectures about child development – a group self-selected to be interested in small human beings. A silvered paediatrician, Janet, grandmothered him effusively and gave me an office as a nursing room. Sated and content, he sat on my knee as the week's speaker delivered the seminar. In his view the talking was entirely for his benefit. He proffered his face-splitting smile, burbled his appreciation. Outside, the sunlight slanted through the square panes of the windows, lancing through motes of dust.

In later years there was a kowhai tree in the garden, grown from a seed brought by Martin Richards from New Zealand when he visited, and nurtured in soil twelve thousand miles from its origin. The few people who recognised a kowhai in Cambridge would stop, startled by the juxtaposition of a southern hemisphere tree glowing lemon and lime against a five-hundred-year-old building. It was an unusual connection between an ancient part of Britain and the new world of New Zealand.

* * *

On a March Saturday morning, Simon, Emily, Alexander and I boarded a British Rail train from Baldock station to King's Cross. Spring sun glanced across the undulations of the fields to the east, stretching its tepid warmth to our feet on the platform. Simon was in charge of the baby buggy; he grew taller with the responsibility, his seven-year-old face solemn as he folded the buggy to get into the carriage. We sang the song Emily and Simon had composed for Alexander: 'Eeh er man he has two feet to walk down the stre-e-et!' It was their song – four- and six-year-olds are idiosyncratic composers. They based it on his most prolific vocalisation – 'Eeh er' - the happy chant of a three-month-old baby. In London our voices soared up toward the rafters in King's Cross Station and bounced back down to us. We moved, a mini-parade, from the main platform down the stairs to the Underground and caught the Piccadilly Line west.

We were a happy quartet on our excursion to Barbara's and Iain's house in West London. Jim was at a meeting, and planned to meet us there later in the day; in the evening he and I were going with Barbara and Iain to a restaurant to celebrate being in the same city together.

As we left King's Cross, Simon and Emily sat side-by-side in the underground carriage, legs dangling, studying the other passengers. A woman sitting opposite smiled at my excited children; her persistent attention was a contrast with the usual English reticence about engaging with strangers in trains. Maternal pride vied with wariness in me – a child had been abducted recently in London. The woman beamed especially beguiling smiles toward Emily, and my gregarious princess reciprocated.

Emily would be the last to get off at the station where we changed lines – 'Mind the gap,' I had said, echoing the disembodied voice from the loud speakers. I climbed down first, Alexander secured under one arm and baby bags swinging from the other. Simon followed with the buggy. I turned to steady him and Emily waited behind him. The doors began to close and she drew back – into the arms of the woman I had persuaded myself might be a child-snatcher. Emily's face blurred and sharpened, blurred again in the window of the train as the carriage lurched and began its slide out of the underground station. Like a dream slipping from one's grasp when you wake in the morning, she slid from my view. As the train glided away along the lines into the tunnel I could see the woman smiling and gesticulating.

Time stopped, and I was motionless with it. My left arm circled Alexander, his infant body pressed against my side. The paraphernalia that accompanies babies swung in the bag slung from my right shoulder. My right hand clutched Simon, who was holding the folded baby buggy. We three stood, an immobilised tableau, as Emily slipped west out of our lives.

Simon looked up at me. His brown eyes pooled with tears. 'It's all your fault!' The four words sliced through me, hot knives into my sense of maternal fitness, which at that moment was plunging into free-fall. He was right – I had committed the most heinous of parental crimes and lost a child.

The Saturday midday platform was dreary and thinly populated by a miscellany of travellers. Groups of young men were coming and going from football matches. Senior citizens hobbled along the platform on Saturday outings. Families stared at the information board, children swinging from their fathers' hands. In the muddle of bodies I saw a uniform that bespoke Underground authority and I moved, dragging my appendages, to engage the person inside the grey-black garb.

'My daughter - she's in that train - the doors closed on her!' I pointed at the tunnel, where Emily and the train had disappeared.

He was Irish, his face callow and pimpled. He struggled to understand my down-under vowels. A couple of repetitions later, he went to an official phone hanging on a hook in a box. My comprehension of his Irish brogue was as challenging as his understanding of my voice – my ears heard a version of English that made no sense. He picked up the phone, I hung on his words, and slowly understood that he was calling through to the next stop and asking for someone there to look out for Emily.

He put the receiver back in its cradle, grey on grimy grey. His demeanour gelled into something resembling a mix of disapproval and impatience. I was clearly irresponsible, should not be in charge of children, and possibly should be reported to the authorities. In the meantime, though, he would improve the life of my poor, poor son by putting money into a machine and handing him chocolate bars. Simon was astounded. Chocolate was for rare and special occasions – maybe this was one of those. He took the bars, looked at me as I rocked Alexander, summed up the situation, and ate two at once. The dispenser of chocolate threw words across his shoulder at me from time to time; I nodded, hoping that yes was an appropriate response. Perhaps he was telling me how I should be raising my children.

Eastbound, westbound, trains scurried through the station, none of them discharging Emily. People poured or lolled or strolled or hurried off. There were no four-year-old girls with or without adult companions. Simon, the buggy, Alexander and I followed the Irishman around the platform like ducklings attached to the wrong mother.

The phone on the platform rang. Our rescuer answered. His gestures and vowels sent in my direction conveyed the message that a woman was bringing Emily back on the eastbound train. As the next one drew in I scanned the people coming off for a female, possibly in railway uniform, returning my child.

In the stream of people decanting from the train, I saw Emily. She trotted towards us, hand-in-hand with the putative child-snatcher, looking up at her, chatting. She and Margaret – for that was her name, Emily told me later – were friends. Then she saw me, and her bravado collapsed. We both wept, she with the pureness of relief and me with an uncomfortable mix of relief and guilt. I had misjudged Angel Margaret. The Irishman melted away and I swamped Margaret with gratitude until she walked off down the platform to catch the westbound train again.

That might have been the end; a lesson to be learned by the irresponsible mother who should have known how to protect her children. Alas, no. We four, as burdened as when we started but now subdued, boarded a Piccadilly Line train to get us to Islington. Emily and I were super-glued together, grasping each other's hands, while baby Alexander wobbled in my other arm. Simon was still taking care of the buggy.

Limbs and bodies squeezed against us in this carriage. Passengers looked at the floor or gazed at the straps their hands were holding, avoiding the risk of eye contact. Simon and Emily were crushed up against me, arms around whatever part they could reach. Alexander was awake and looking over my shoulder, wide-eyed and smiling the indiscriminate grin of a three-month-old, bestowing it on everyone within range. A whiskered face smelling of stale ale started pushing itself closer to his, and a bony finger rose up from the melee of limbs below and coochy-cooed him under his chin. My baby beamed, encouraging his admirer to further intimacies. I pulled Alexander back into me as far as I could, willing our stop to come quickly.

The train's brakes screeched, metal scraping on unoiled metal, and we pushed through to the door, buggy preceding us, and clambered off, hooked together like the links of an unwieldy chain. Simon opened out the buggy on the platform. Still pasted to Emily, I wriggled Alexander down into his seat and strapped him in. Simon was reaching up for the buggy handles to start the voyage down the platform to the 'Way Out' sign, when Alexander's be-whiskered admirer appeared beside him and grabbed the handles.

'Let me push him for you, sonny.' It was the first time I had heard his voice, apart from the universally accented coochy coo. Another Irishman, this one relaxed with alcohol. He set off along the platform, my tiny son in front and my larger one trotting behind.

We ran to keep up. 'Thank you,' I said, 'I can manage from here.' We came, an unlikely convoy, to the barriers and I grabbed the handles of the buggy, thanking the man again for his help. He put his face down close to Alexander's, gave him a kiss and me a beatific gappy smile, and shambled off in the direction of the pub near the station.

At Barbara and Iain's house, Simon and Emily clambered around the kitchen table with their small cousin Anna, eating fish fingers and drinking orange juice. Alexander snuggled into his portable sheepskin, sated with his last feed of the day. Jim appeared, and I blurted out what had happened, my words saturated with guilt and relief as he came through the door. A babysitter arrived, and the four of us set out for the Robert Carrier restaurant for dinner. We meandered to the tube station, Jim and me arm-in-arm, and caught a train to the restaurant.

As we sat down, my anticipation was tainted with self-blame. Other possible outcomes chased themselves through my imagination like puppies in a forest. What if Emily had not been returned? What if the inebriated Irishman had outrun Simon and Emily and me, with Alexander in his pushchair? The arrival of a picturesque plate of duck with cassis sauce quietened my self-recriminations.

As Jim toasted me for being a first-class master of science he toasted, too, our being good-enough parents.

I was exonerated from carelessness of the worst kind, for letting Emily be carried away on the underground and for failing to stop a drunk run off down the platform with Alexander. It took me a lot longer to forgive myself.

There were, of course, consequences. Three years later, Emily and I were waiting for a lift to open its doors, doors not dissimilar to those of an underground train, and transport us up three floors in a multi-storey building in New Zealand. Her hand trembled in mine, held it tighter. As the doors squealed open she said, 'Let's walk up the stairs, Mummy.' Of course!

'Good idea,' I said.

Eight

Visiting Europe from New Zealand entails a major exercise in travelling that includes long flights and several weeks in hand. The energy and resources needed are discouraging, especially for those encumbered by small children. The ease of doing the same from England was one of the main attractions of being there for a year. In early April on a Friday night, after a trip across the English Channel on a ferry, the five of us settled into a hotel in Paris.

For Simon and Emily the excitement of the weekend that had already started on the journey over was kept in flow by the hotel lift. It was a tantalising arrangement of doors and grilles, with space for us all only if we squeezed together as if we were in an underground carriage in rush hour. It had two doors, an outer grille contraption and an inner steel plate. The lift refused to move if they were not both fastened, a feature that we discovered after several attempts to persuade it to elevate five humans and their baggage. It clanged to our fourth-floor level, spilled us out into an unlit hallway.

'I want to do it again.' Simon pulled the handle of the grille back and forth.

'I want to do it, too.' Emily had her turn while parents and baggage and baby waited.

We found the door to our room, and Simon and Emily rushed in to explore. They found their beds, and discovered a bidet in the bathroom.

'What's that for, Daddy?'

'It is for washing your bottom after you've been to the toilet.'

They dubbed it the 'washbottom'.

The two rooms were minuscule, but we did not mean to spend much time in them. We were there to adventure in the city. The windows had bars on them, and looked down on to what we imagined was a typical Paris street. It was a corridor, an exotic jumble of cafés and *boulangeries*, and Parisians talking fast to each other. Their decibel level was high above that of the restrained English conversing we had become accustomed to in Hertfordshire.

I fed Alexander and we reversed the procedure we'd been through coming in, closing the lift doors in order and clanking down to get out into the street for our first exploration.

Alexander was in his folding pushchair, regarding the adult world with his brown eyes at knee-level.

We found the nearest Metro station, where the four of us each took a corner of the pushchair and swung him down the steps. He flew up and down in his baby throne, carried by his admirers. Simon and Emily sang to him. 'Eeh er man he has two feet to walk down the stre-e-et!'

Two days later, the wind in the Bois de Bologne was sharp, slicing into tiny lungs. Alexander was sick. He lay limp in his father's arms, not hungry, not singing. He did not want to feed, and he drooped against my chest as I held him back in the hotel room. I felt shards of worry - he was hot. While Simon and Emily and Jim went up the Eiffel Tower, I took Alexander to a doctor, who prescribed a list of irrelevant medications including suppositories. They were, it seemed, a staple of French prescriptions. But the list included an antibiotic. We spooned the sticky fluid into Alexander's mouth and in a few hours he livened up. He started feeding. He smiled, he sang, he was himself again.

Across the road from the hotel was a small local café. We five wandered in, Alexander asleep under my coat. As we wriggled into the small spaces around the table, he woke and wanted more milk. I covered him with my coat; how would Parisians feel about breastfeeding in public? The owner approached our table, apron tied across his expansive tummy. '*Bonjour, Monsieur*,' said Jim in his confident but partial French. He fell back into English for: 'We are ready to order.' The maître d' saw Alexander nestled under my jacket, heard his snuffling, turned and walked away. Perhaps he was offended. He came back a minute later, trailed by his wife and two children, all there to admire *le bébé*.

The French love children, the English love dogs.

* * *

We were back in Bygrave. Three children, five of us, tight five, happy five. We felt complete. Jim and I decided that for us fertility was obsolete, and troublesome to control. To change that, one of us would need to succumb to the ministrations of a surgeon's knife.

'How do you feel about having a vasectomy?' I asked Jim.

The subtle blanching of his face conveyed just how he felt. Despite performing this small surgery on patients himself, he was uneasy about having his generative capacity curtailed. There is both a physical and a metaphysical component to men's hesitations about vasectomies.

Three pregnancies had wrought havoc with my ligaments. No longer was mine the taut body of a childless young woman; my insides were sagging. So I was content with the prospect of having no more babies. I had time, lashings of time, and no abstract misgivings. Minor surgery was nothing to worry about. It was agreed – I would have my tubes tied.

On Thursday 9th April, four days after getting back from Paris, I kissed Simon and Emily goodbye as they climbed onto the school bus then I fastened Alexander into the baby car seat, and drove down the A1 to the Queen Charlotte Hospital in London. I was there to be booked for the surgery for a tubal ligation.

Alexander bounced on my knee as I talked to the gynaecologist in the outpatients department. He swung on my hip as we walked down the graceless hospital corridors to the gynaecology ward. He was to come into hospital with me while I had the surgery. He charmed the gynaecology staff, who organised a cot to be beside my bed while we were there, and the date was set. It was to be the following Monday, 13th April, four days away.

In her Chiswick garden that afternoon, Barbara dandled Alexander on her lap. Her physiotherapist hands moved gently around his back. She listened to his lungs.

'I can't believe this baby had bronchiolitis a few days ago.'

He grinned at her, his eyes crinkling with the waves of his smile.

After lunch in Barbara's garden, he and I drove back up the A1 to Bygrave in time to greet the children from school. It was a warm spring Thursday afternoon.

Nine

Somewhere, in the depths of that little being was a fatal flaw, an imperfection that allowed him to die – suddenly, quietly – and painlessly? If I could pray, I would beg that he did not know he could not breathe, that he did not struggle with fright and panic and awareness that something was wrong. I want to believe that his last awareness was of wriggling sensuously down on his sheepskin, wrapped in a soft shawl, going lazily to sleep after the exertion of laughing and delighting in the sunlight and filling his tummy with milk... Diary, April 1981

The undertaker's viewing room smelled sweet and sour – preservative and death vied for the attention of our noses. There was just enough space for four or five adults to lean around a person-sized casket. The air was still, unbreathing. Two of us and a baby-sized white coffin left expanses of space along the edges of the room; space filled with grey silence. Other people's grief permeated the off-white walls, layer on layer of sadness left by mourners passing through.

A child's coffin has to be small to hold its young inhabitant. In front of us was a toy casket, a truncated tomb. Its lid lay beside it. Our baby lay inside it.

There had been a post-mortem. Legally, it had to happen, since no one could tell why he had died. An anonymous pathologist had sliced into Alexander's tiny body, examined his heart and lungs, his kidneys and his liver, and his brain. The search was for clues to explain his death. I hoped that compassion was in the hand that held the knife. That the person probing for an explanation felt sadness as she opened him up and exposed the parts of him that no-one else would see. That the pathologist would feel frustration and helplessness as she failed to find answers. And that he or she restored his body gently, as best she could to its public shape, stitching the wounds and hiding the evidence of reluctant violation.

I looked for incisions from the pathologist's knife, and saw nothing. The pathologist had done her job well. And Alexander had been embalmed. We were not asked whether we wanted his body preserved. Maybe embalming has to be done when a post-mortem is carried out. Or maybe *not* embalming a body was not considered as an alternative at the time.

An embalmed body is confusing, distressing in its distorted image of the live person. Alexander looked like a wax model. His body had been drained of its own fluids and filled with preservative. There in the coffin was a physical resemblance to our baby; a still, cold replica of the crying, warm, vital and wriggling small person we had known. Twenty-four hours ago we had held that stilled body, warm and soft in our arms. Still, but real. Now all we had was this plastic lookalike. It was cold, it was hard, and we did not have it for long.

How should we farewell our dead baby? The question opened up on itself, expanded and unfolded, multilayered and soaked in distress. A death demands action and we had decisions we had to make. The need for action flailed against the torpor of our brains and bodies. The craving to go to bed and weep was compelling.

Above all, Simon and Emily needed our support and our explanations. In those days between Alexander's death and the funeral, all we could do was to hold them, tell them in our words – but not necessarily in ways that they understood – that Alexander had died, that he would not be coming back, that we had to get through the next days and weeks together.

'We could bury him near Bygrave,' Jim said. 'Or somewhere… maybe London?' He did not sound convinced.

'Who would look after his grave? Who would remember him, who would visit him?'

I imagined Alexander lying unrecognised, unacknowledged, in a corner of a cemetery visited only by us and only if we came back to England. Passers-by wandering in the cemetery might, for a moment, inhale the smell of desolation seeping from a small, unkempt grave and wonder whose baby lay there. The moment would pass and they would walk on. The thought of strangers' pity was painful. The thought of abandoning his body was worse.

We decided to have him cremated.

The gathering place in the Westminster area of London for bodies to be cremated is Mortlake Crematorium. It is described today on Wikipedia as a "rare example of Art Deco design, a building of exceptional design and character", and "probably the most undiscovered deco treasure in London". Crematoria as Art Deco treasures seems an unlikely juxtaposition, and in 1981 its significance was lost on us. We did not raise our eyes to gaze at that celebrated ceiling.

We focused on what had to be done, as automatons might. We chose a day, we booked a time. We took the shortest time-slot available. We had no idea what we were going to do, how we would fill even those few minutes.

We had no scripts, no guidance about how to do his funeral.

Despite my opportunist pleas to potential saviours when he was dying, one thing we were certain about – we did not want to add hypocrisy to distress by having a service taken by a member of the clergy. If there were secular celebrants available then, we did not know about them and the crematorium offered us no information about alternative ceremonies. We had no wise person to hold and guide us through this stricken, unfamiliar territory. So it was up to us. Somehow, we managed to sign the necessary papers, and to complete the arrangements with the crematorium. The mortician, it seemed, would deliver Alexander's body in its coffin to the site at the time we had chosen.

We did know that we wanted to have some music to play at his funeral. We floundered - how to choose, what to choose? As distracted parents of young children we had lost track of current ballads and songs. We had spent several years being deaf to what was being played on popular radio. But we did listen to chamber music. In the three days between his death and his funeral we looked for solace in what we knew. We chose the first movement of Beethoven's *String Quartet Opus 131*. I do not know how we came to this choice; I do know that as soon as we played it we knew at a visceral level that it was right. And we did not know then that Richard Wagner had described the first movement as "revealing the most melancholy sentiment expressed in music". Beethoven himself regarded the quartet as his greatest. Our inarticulate intuitions were both accurate and shared.

The chapel was a cavern; a cold space distressingly inappropriate for the size of the tiny body we were farewelling. Business was brisk at Mortlake that day. Our turn came and we moved to the front, four of us, two by two. Simon's and Emily's hands were fastened to ours. There was the slight white coffin, diminutive in the spaciousness, in the gloom, encompassing our baby. It was on a stand meant for an adult coffin. It looked ineffably alone, awash in the sorrow of the chapel.

After Alexander

There was a straggle of family with us. Two sisters and their husbands. They had known and held Alexander. Jim's parents, Esther and Jim senior, had arrived from New Zealand too late to meet their new grandchild. How doubly hollowed they must have felt – they had never held him, and now he was lost.

Ten of us, huddled in the front row of an area built to hold 150 mourners.

Jim went first to the podium, and talked about his baby son. He stood tall, proud, weeping as he spoke of his love for Alexander. I went next, stumbling and shaking. My words were written on a crumpled piece of cardboard:

Alexander came to us bringing joy and love and laughter. He was the focus of happiness in the family, and his joy reached out to touch the lives of friends and strangers, from Parisian maids to alcoholics on the underground.

He was our breakfast time conversationalist, our companion on walks, our friend for pub lunches. He smiled through the winter and laughed in the spring. He was our Pigeon, our Little Man. A loving and beloved baby, he leaves a pool of silence in our hearts.

It did not take long. It was the least and the most I could manage.

Our voices struggled to drift the few metres to the ears of our family in front of us. Simon's and Emily's faces were dazed, as they tried to make sense of what was happening around them. The adults they adored, the grown-ups on whom they relied for support, were incoherent.

Then Beethoven spoke for us, picked us up and took us over.

The opening movement of *Opus 131* is fulsome with sorrow. It dirged our grief. Toward its end, it lifted. It spoke of hope from the darkest places, of warmth in the coldest crevasses, it ascended to the high spaces in the roof of that building. It sang redemption, it sang courage, it sang love. The sun came slanting through the chapel windows.

Our time was over. Someone dressed in black pushed a button. The coffin started creeping toward the end of the plinth. The body of our baby was carried along in its blanched box until it slid through a screen to the opening of the furnace beyond. We watched the physical remnants of our child disappear. We stood unmoving, focused on the closing screen, until another black-clad assistant took our elbows, ushered us out. The next body was ready. We went out into the sun, blinking.

Outside the crematorium, Emily held my hand. Her face was still, her green-grey eyes looked up at the chimney. It reared into the sky, a concrete pillar with straggles of white smoke coming from its top. She was waiting for a white coffin to come out and go up into the blueness above. Simon stood with Jim, father's and son's faces as pale as the sides of the coffin.

After Alexander

We drifted away from the crematorium with the rest of the family, arms wrapped around shoulders and hands held tightly, bodies ebbing and flowing together and apart in the warmth of the day. There was nothing and everything to say, everything and nothing to do. Alexander was gone, his body transformed to ash. He was irretrievable. A hole the shape and size of a baby gaped and ached in my insides. We meandered along London streets, found our way to the banks of the Thames. We sat on sun-warmed steps, leaned against each other, watched the river slide by. In the tree above us a London blackbird sang his song.

Ten

We had not been able to think of a better way to say goodbye to Alexander. The funeral lacked structure, it lacked ceremony, and it failed as a ritual. It was unfinished, our farewells muffled and unfocused.

In the Anglican Church, the *Common Book of Prayer* dictates that a priest should say upon the death of a child:

> O God, whose beloved Son did take little children into his arms and bless them: Give us grace, we beseech thee, to entrust this child *N.* to thy never-failing care and love, and bring us all to thy heavenly kingdom; through the same thy Son Jesus Christ our Lord, who liveth and reigneth with thee and the Holy Spirit, one God, now and for ever. *Amen.*

For Christians, these words must be reassuring. God has taken their child into His care, and He understands their situation – His son has also died, and is now with Him. And so our child can be. For those of us who do not hold the faith, they offer no comfort. We could not bring ourselves, even in our grief, to murmur these words or to have them said for us. The scripts provided by churches were meaningless to us. Yet we had nothing else to say in their place.

We were caught in the ebb tide of formal ritual. God and his churches were on the wane. Secular rituals had not been developed to fill the void that was expanding as the church was losing its power to hold the grieving. There was little to reassure the increasing numbers of doubters such as we were.

As young adults in the Seventies we had felt no need for ritual in our lives. We had dipped ourselves into encounter groups and emerged dampened with self-awareness. Meaning and ritual were made up in the moment, depending on the scan of feelings we were experiencing. Lack of formality was the zeitgeist. The fluctuating Seventies and their teenage counterparts, the Swinging Sixties, had freed themselves and us from the shackles of ceremony. We were intoxicated by the freedoms, we rejected structure. Ritual was confining. We were shedding traditional cultural and religious beliefs and replacing them with spontaneity. And because our parents were alive and healthy, our children young and vibrant, we had no reason then to confront the need for the comfort of ceremony, the consolation of ritual.

Now we had fallen into a barren place. It was the gap between religiously framed and increasingly irrelevant ceremony, and the undeveloped and elusive secular framework of a non-religious funeral. The secular ceremonies that might have been available had we known about them would have lacked the grounding of experience. They ran the risk of being superficial, of being bereft of legitimacy. It would take some years for secular funerals to achieve the validity that church-based ceremonies held. We needed a framework for releasing Alexander, and we did not have one. So we had made do with our own home-grown, ritual-free, comfortless efforts. If he had died today we would have had an authentic non-religious framework for farewelling him that could offer both comfort and authenticity.

Nearly four decades later, secular celebrants help grieving friends and family members to take a path in their leave-taking rituals that gives consolation and comfort without recourse to religious belief. It is a delicate undertaking, one which effective celebrants do with grace and compassion.

* * *

The belief in some form of life after death consoles both the dying and the bereaved, and it is a belief that continues to give consolation both within and outside religious settings. In secular spiritual settings, mediums flourish, offering to connect the grieving living with the dead. Relationships with beloved lost ones are encouraged and sustained, conversations are fostered and mediated.

My lack of belief in life after death brings with it the danger of putting me into a bleak zone. It is not bleak, however, because the memory of Alexander, held by me and a few others, *is* his life after death.

Paul Auster, in his memoir of his father *The Invention of Solitude*[2], quotes poem fragments from Mallarmé written about the death of his son.

no – nothing
to do with the great
deaths – etc.
    -    as long as we
go on living, he
lives – in us.

It will only be after our
death that he will be dead
    -    and the bells
of the Dead will toll
                  Stéphane Mallarmé's *Fragment 28*

People who die stay in the memories of people who loved and knew them, whether or not those left behind believe in an

---

[2] Paul Auster: *The Invention of Solitude*. Faber and Faber, 2012. Pp 117-118.

afterlife. We do not forget our parents, children, and friends, although our exact recollections of them undoubtedly transform and blur over time. There is a sense, then, of Alexander – for example – existing as a potent memory in the heads and hearts of Jim and me, and the few others that knew him. We may or may not pool those memories. And, as Mallarmé indicates, they are not passed on to another generation. The memories, and therefore that way of continuing to exist, die with those who hold them. That seems somehow appropriate, and far more real than the difficult notion of an afterlife somewhere else.

It also raises the intriguing notion that a funeral for an individual might also be the acknowledgement of the final dying of those people whom that person held as memories when no-one else remained to do so. In practice it is virtually impossible to know who they might be. Nonetheless, it is a multilayered aspect of a funeral that may be acknowledged by celebrants and others who officiate.

I find this perspective on existence after death deeply satisfying. Memory feels more immediate, and much more accessible than an improbable and unimaginable existence beyond dying.

* * *

Recently the eleven-year-old grandson of a friend died. He had succumbed to leukaemia after a battle that no child should have to wage. His family and his school had enabled him to live a flourishing life until very soon before he died. The funeral ceremony was a tender and contemporary blend of religious ceremony and personal tribute, an example of how funerals have developed as authentic reflections of the life and loss of a child.

The priest conducting the funeral was glorious. Shining Samoan skin against the whitest of white robes, the serenity of a believer, a large gentleness and a voice that hugged the mourners. The prayers had been said, the eulogies sung through the church and filtered out through the modern glass windows; the photo montage had played to the accompaniment of songs that triggered open weeping for this child.

The priest stood behind the child's coffin. For a moment his serenity deserted him, his voice faltered. 'Goodbye, Geordie, you are in God's care now.' He knew this boy, his grief had for an instant overcome his consolation that Geordie was in a better place.

'You have made me the best person I can be,' said Geordie's mother, eloquent through her tears. 'When you were born I wondered if we would like each other, but we did. I love you passionately.'

His father bent over to reach the microphone and, strong through his tears, gave his speech. He talked of Geordie's humour, his living in the present, his enjoyment of life, of his happiness being greatest when others were happy.

His school principal told of Geordie's strong personality, his charm as he ensured that things went his way. His teacher noted his facility with the magical words 'I love you'. He told of how Geordie brought a sense of reality to the classroom when he greeted a ten-minute speech given by the teacher with: 'blah, blah, blah.'

Children and their parents filed up to write on the coffin. Their words would perish in the fire with the casket and Geordie's small body, reduced by leukaemia to a shadow. The writing was done with care, mouths of children moving with the movements of the pens, adults bending to write out their sorrow and their farewells. It is doubtful that anyone believed that Geordie would receive their outpourings, yet they wrote as if they did. This was a ritual that by-passed the priest's passage of ceremony. He stood in the aisle, watching. He rocked gently.

A boy entered the church from the back, stick legs supporting his body, playing a grown-up set of bagpipes whose keening cut through the murmuring. He walked to the front of the coffin, emulating the straight leg movements he had seen in adult bagpipers. He marched in time to his dirge. He turned. He led the small assemblage of pallbearers, and the dead boy in his box, out of the church. A haka, a Maori chant, started up, lusty voices of fifteen European ten-year-olds honouring their school friend. The coffin slid into a white hearse, balloons leapt into the sky.

* * *

Too late for Alexander, funerals have been transformed. Even those held in churches, like Geordie's, include eulogies ranging from brief life summaries given by priests to rambling and often funny accounts of the person's life given by friends and family members. They are personal, they are authentic, and they embody ritual that is immediate and real.

I will forever regret that we did not and could not farewell Alexander so fully, coherently, and passionately. If I could go back in time and create a funeral for him, how would it be?

It would be in a garden; a garden he had loved and shared with birds – especially blackbirds.

All who love us and him, potentially or actually, would be there.

A gentle and wise person would take us by the hearts and lead us through his ceremony.

Words would be spoken that expressed his unique self, his joy, his laughter and his love.

There would be no limit on the time taken to farewell him.

* * *

The garbled ceremony for Alexander was insufficient for us and, although we failed to realise it then, it was also unsatisfying for other family members.

Seven years later, Alexander's paternal grandfather died. His funeral was held in a Presbyterian Church in Auckland, presided over by a minister.

As the organ climbed its opening crescendo and slid gently down to silence, the family sat in the front pews of a church that smelled of warm wood, face powder, shoe polish, and the dust of hymn books.

'We are here to celebrate the lives of James Michael Watt, and of Alexander John Watt,' said the Minister.

My body tensed. His addition of Alexander was unexpected and, for an instant, confronting. Then astonishment at hearing Alexander's name transformed into gratitude for his inclusion in this ceremony, despite my secular stance. The ritual of farewelling him with his grandfather with dignity and traditional rites felt like a sustaining conclusion, if not the one we would have chosen. The deep consolation of ritual overcame the discomfort at his inclusion in a Christian service. I do not know who decided to name him in this ceremony so many years later. Perhaps his grandmother, my beloved mother-in-law who had been in London for the ten minutes of farewell at the crematorium, had asked the Presbyterian Minister to dedicate this ceremony to both. It was a deferred completion for me and, I think, for Jim.

Eleven

Now, in England, what we had were his ashes.

When you bury a body, you are left with a place – a space in the ground dedicated to the body that is consigned to it. The body's location is marked with a stone, a symbol that indicates who the person is, and sometimes a few facts about them. It is a place that endures, with rare exceptions.

When someone is cremated, you have their ashes, or more accurately a residue of bone and coffin. What were we to do with Alexander's ashes?

We had driven back to Mortlake Crematorium to collect them. They were handed over in a polystyrene box that had neither gravitas nor grace. We had decided not to buy one of the ornate containers on offer from the crematorium – ornate was not our style, and there was nothing available between stark and opulent. A simple wooden box or a strong, plain cardboard container would have been more soothing than the cool fakery of what was on offer.

We held what was left of our baby. He felt light, insubstantial, as if he would fly away if we loosened our grip. We passed him between us, relinquishing him carefully to the hands of the other. The juxtaposition of synthetic white foam with the weight of our sadness was painful. We took him home to Bygrave.

We needed to do something with these ill-clad ashes as soon as possible – either find an appropriate container, or decide on some other future for them.

We did not want to keep them on a mantelpiece, or in a drawer, or behind glass in a cabinet. Those options did not just seem repellent; they were also impractical, as we were returning to New Zealand. For reasons still mysterious, the Ministry of Agriculture and Fisheries had decreed that we could not take human ashes home. Neither could we post them; they simply were not allowed into the country. Who knew what plagues and infections might result if a box of human remains arrived in New Zealand from a foreign state like England? The Ministry officials were not interested in making an exception and we lacked the energy for a fight.

And so we decided to entrust them to the sea. On the long wooden table in the Bygrave house we opened out a map of Britain. The island was there before us, the shape of a dragon foetus curling around the egg of Ireland. Nowhere is far from the sea, as the blackbird flies. We measured with our eyes - the eastern coast looked the most accessible from Hertfordshire. We chose a place called Stiffkey - pronounced Stewkey, following the same kind of inscrutable logic that sees so many English places pronounced with little resemblance to how the word looks. Who, other than an English person, would know that Magdalene is pronounced Maudlin? Or that Worcester is Wuster? Stiffkey, Stewkey, neither is particularly mellifluous. But it was close and it had easy access to the sea.

Stiffkey is six miles east of a town named Wells-next-the-Sea. We did not know then that the village of Stiffkey achieved a kind of notoriety in the early twentieth century, when the 'Randy Rector of Stiffkey' held office there at St John's Church. Harold Davidson was appointed after an early life that was unorthodox for the son of a vicar. Rather than falling in with his father's desire that he train in holy orders, he had been drawn to the theatre. He was finally persuaded by his father to study at Oxford. He was appointed to Stiffkey by the Marquess Townshend, who was the patron of two parishes, in gratitude for mediating a dispute between his family and himself when he married a woman deemed inappropriate by them.

In 1932, Davidson was defrocked for unconventional behaviour. He was prone to going to the rescue of prostitutes in London. He did not, though, go without resistance. The community was divided in its support for him and when he was locked out of the church he held services in front of it, attracting over a thousand parishioners for his final sermon. This was a group at least four times the size of the whole town of Stiffkey; his admirers had congregated from far beyond its confines.

Today, Stiffkey has 223 inhabitants, and a fine camping ground. We decided to camp for the weekend, and to take the ashes to the shoreline there. We crammed the tent and mad Muffin into the boot of the car; Simon and Emily, the ashes and camp food went into the back seat, and we headed out for the coast.

There was no road that took a straight line to the sea. We struck out north-east, meandering along B roads between hedgerows chiming with birdsong. We skirted the traffic jams encircling the edges of Cambridge, we drove past Ely Cathedral with its feet in the fens and its tower reaching for the sky.

'Did you know I went to a concert there once and the conductor fainted?' I said to the children. 'The first violinist held him up until he recovered and the orchestra played on.'

Silence from the back seat.

'He was famous. His name was Daniel Barenboim.'

Polite murmurs from behind me. They continued reading their books; I do not know how they can read when they are in a moving car.

'How are you doing in the back, darlings?'

'Okay.'

Isn't the countryside lovely?'

Silence.

After Alexander

Eastern England was marvellously, understatedly, lovely. Low-slung church towers grazed between low-hanging sky and flat land, the lines between diffuse. There was a harmony of water, land and sky that was satisfyingly coherent.

It also holds mysteries, a blend of ancient Scandinavian pagan religion and Christianity. I had written a poem about Suffolk once before when I was in England.

Silver sky drapes the shoulders of the land,
hunched against its mass.
There's no hiding; you dream her
before she finds you.

Hazed light mutes the gaze, shrouds the land
in discretion. This sky
embraces sun and moon together; double whammy
using soft focus to evade scrutiny.

Sprawled feet of land dabbling in the water,
reeds between the toes. Trees duck their heads
against the sky; martello towers squat
obediently, church towers offer it no challenge.

When we reached Stiffkey I read this to Simon and Emily. There was not even the damning of faint praise.

The dubious poetry of mothers is especially boring when you are seven and five. Back to their own books.

The tent was old. Jim and I wrestled with poles and ropes, confusing back with front. The children and Muffin raced around the camping ground, exploring its perimeter. The salt marshes were just beyond its edge, glistening pale pink as light faded from the sky. The tent encompassed the four of us in a taut frame, holding our sadness close. It engulfed us as we went to sleep, the ashes in their flimsy box at the end of our stretchers. Muffin was put in the car to sleep, wailing her indignation at not being in the tent with us.

In the morning the sun rose over the marshes, tinted rose and sloping toward the tent. We walked toward the beach on a ribbon of path that navigated an expanse of black mud, purple flowers, stunted shrubs and rapturous birds, stretching out between the land and the sea. Footbridges built like church arches spanned the expanses of water. Simon and Emily climbed their sides and threw stones down into the pools. We jumped puddles, Muffin put up birds, her nose quivering in doggy hope of capturing a mouthful of feathers. The light was low, fine, warm, tender. The beach stretched, languid and deserted.

The walk back to the tent for breakfast was as subdued as the air.

Jim played cricket with the children while the dog ran mindless circuits, taking approximate swipes at the ball. Inside the tent, I made coffee. I was waiting, heart tumbling at the finality of dispersing the meagre remains of Alexander. I wanted it to be over even as a shred of me clung to the irrationality that clutching that polystyrene container was still to be holding him. Whatever was in there had to be relinquished.

After breakfast we made our way back through the saline flats to the beach, Jim carrying Alexander's ashes in the light white box. Simon and Emily were silent, not leaping puddles as they had before breakfast but walking in a line with Jim and me along the path which meandered amongst the squat bushes and the glistening pools of marsh water. Muffin failed to attune to the atmosphere; she resumed her search for prey in the bushes.

The moment, when it came, was muted. The four of us took handfuls of silver-grey dust and put them in the sea. The remnants of our baby swirled with the waves, out a little way then back to the shore, close to our feet. Gradually, they dispersed, moving out to the larger sea beyond. I imagined a current running directly from the beach, out through nearby Blakeney Harbour mouth and down across the equator, past Australia to Cook Strait in New Zealand, through the entrance to Queen Charlotte Sound and up to Anakiwa, to the feet of the family bach. He would join us there, I fancied. Maybe, just maybe, a fragment of his remains would make it home. Simon and Emily wrote his name in large letters in the sand. By the next tide they had gone.

We drove home. There were just four of us.

Twelve

When the blackbird flew out of sight
It marked the edge
Of one of many circles
Summer Morning Stanza IX, Wallace Stevens

Where there is death you will often find God. Many of those who profess not to be religious will still, as they experience the loss of someone they love, say that they believe there is something out there, beyond here, over yonder past the crematorium or grave that engulfs the remains of their beloved. They do not always call whatever it is God, but that is what they mean, or something like it. Their loss generates a form of faith that was not there before.

Others may reject their existing belief in God or a god, a faith that they have held until the point where they lose someone they love. It becomes impossible for them to have faith in a deity that would allow their beloved to die.

Death, then, can strengthen an existing belief in God, or it may provoke the resurrection of an old one. The consolation offered by religious belief can be compelling. It pervades condolences from the explicitly scriptural to the vaguest reassurances of divine compassion. And it usually includes, implicitly or overtly, some form of trust that there is existence after death.

Or, a death can extinguish faith.

Neither of these happened for me. There was no resurrection of former belief, and nor did I reject an existing one. My voyage through religious education and ensuing belief had started in childhood, and finished in a place where consolation had to be sought elsewhere. And now the authenticity of this journey was to be tested.

* * *

When I was a child, my parents were fainthearted Christians. They were not even of the Christmas and Easter variety of church-attenders. I have no memory of conversations with them about the nature of God or His Son, nor how they might be relevant to our lives. At most I was marinaded in a bath of lukewarm Christian principles, unarticulated but assumed. We said grace before meals – *for what we are about to receive, may the Lord make us truly thankful, Amen.* It was an unexamined ritual with the essential message that gratitude is a virtue.

My mother professed a tepid affinity with the Anglican Church, a tie weakened almost fatally by its rejection of her marriage in 1945 to a divorced man. They married instead in the less judgmental Presbyterian House of God down the street. Marriage anywhere other than in a church was not, seventy years ago, a respectable option.

Churches were available to our family and to most in the town, when necessary for events such as marriages and funerals. As some kind of precaution, my parents had me christened – a conformity of sorts as well as a diffuse safeguard. And perhaps under the same impulse of providing insurance, they dropped me at the door of the Presbyterian Hall each week to attend Sunday School. We lined up, a drift of six- to ten-year-olds, waiting to be let in through the doors of the squat wooden building beside the church. My never-cut hair was braided to my waist and decorated with wide, unfashionable ribbons. In tune with the lack of compassion of small girls in small towns, I was teased for this prominent aberration. It was a point of difference easily seized by bored children. Everyone except me had suitably bobbed hair with pretty hair clips. I had no defence; I was outnumbered by girls whose mothers knew what was fashionable.

That ordeal ended as we filed in from the sunlight to the dark room smelling of dust and Bibles, to sit on wooden chairs designed for discomfort, and to sing songs about Jesus loving us; this we knew, because the Bible told us so. Little ones to him belong, we sang, we were weak but he was strong. Yes, Jesus loves me. It meant little to me. I felt quite strong, not weak, and there was no perceptible sign of Jesus' love in that room full of motes. We closed our eyes on command as the austere woman who was leading us prayed. The words she said are long-forgotten, but her fervour lingers. Today, I ponder her passion for God and her determination to infect us with her ardour. Did she, I wonder, have love left over to share with her husband and children?

Shirley, a neighbourhood school friend, had parents who were Christians. Her mother had the same raw-boned face and fervid eyes as the Sunday School teacher. Shirley and I walked to our rural primary school together in the mornings along the side of the roads with no footpaths, swinging our schoolbags. One morning she was unusually animated and at morning talk-time told us, cheeks radiant with rashes of excitement and embarrassment, that the night before her mother and father had announced that they were going to the bedroom and that she and her older sister and brother were to do the dishes. In what was likely to be a rare act of rebellion in such a compliant household, the three children crept along the hallway of their old farmhouse and looked through the keyhole into the bedroom. The details of what they saw were vague in her telling; they understood, however, that the intention was to make a baby.

Passion did not seem to feature in this event, at least in Shirley's description. Keyholes, though, offer limited opportunities for purveying emotions. It was pre-meditated, and apparently successful, as a baby sister was born nine months later. For Shirley and her siblings, it was perhaps not much different from what they witnessed in the paddock when the ram was put with the ewes at tupping time on their farm.

Theirs was a duty performed in the eyes of God (and unintentionally their children), nothing more.

At least Shirley's mother did not make her grow her hair down to her waist.

* * *

The Christian rituals my parents introduced into my childhood were encouraged by the person who became my godmother when I was christened, another ardent and gently cruel Christian woman. Nana Davis was a leftover from my mother's days as a young single woman in Wellington when they both worked for the Red Cross during World War Two. She was pasted into my life and she made sure she was a part of it, because I was her only godchild.

Yearly from the age of four, I was loaded onto a very small plane at Omaka airport in Blenheim. It had one propeller, that looked as if it was made from balsa wood, and it shook its way to Paraparaumu on the edge of the North Island. I was no doubt scared, but it inured me to any fear of flying in small planes. Today I am an intrepid passenger in tiny flying machines that rely on one engine.

Nana Davis would collect me in her grey Morris Minor car and drive me to her house. She was four-feet-ten-inches tall, and praying to her God was her most compelling activity. She was on her knees several times a day. The second most important aspect of her life was the current curate she had boarding with her in her stucco house in Lower Hutt. She always had a curate. A goddaughter came further down the line of importance.

To a four-year-old, the house was mysterious. I had access to the kitchen, an adjoining sitting room where four adults could just fit knee-to-knee – often to read the Bible - and to the front porch of the house, where I slept. Other rooms in the house were closed off; silent, dark spaces that were forbidden regions for a small child.

Well down the chain of relevance in her life was her husband, whom I called Uncle Howard. He was a figure without content; a compliant, silent man who, like me, was not allowed to use the inside toilet. That room was reserved for Nana Davis and the curate. Uncle Howard and I braved spiders and bogeymen in the toilet shed at the back of the house.

Grace before meals was a lengthy and often personal monologue, thanking God for specifics such as my arrival, as well as the usual wide-spanned gratitude for His love. We went to church twice a week, kneeling on cloths that had issued from Nana Davis's crochet hook and hands like tissues from a box.

Idle hands, I was assured, were the devil's playthings. Did the devil cut off our hands, maybe, and put them in his toy box? I tried to keep mine busy, though there wasn't much to do when Nana D was praying.

Her house was opposite the railway station. In 1950 the trains ran on steam. As one approached the station it sounded its whistle, alerting anyone who might not have heard its bellicose approach. The whistle was a demented shriek, driven by coal-induced steam through a valve. My stomach pitched with fear as I lay in the cot bed in the front porch. On the first night I leapt out of bed and ran through to Nana Davis's room. She was on her knees, talking to God, and a frightened four-year-old was not to intrude on the conversation. I had to wait until her communications were finished before I could get her attention.

* * *

At home, the drop-offs to the Sunday School hall became sporadic as we started to spend weekends in the Marlborough Sounds. My parents' sense of duty toward Sunday School had waned as weekends began to be spent at the family's new focus, the bach.

It was at the bach and its surrounds that a sense of awe developed; a gradual grounding of my self in something outside my body. In childhood I did not connect it to someone called God, the person I learned about at Sunday school; rather it was a simple reverence that I still hold for the heart-stopping triumvirate of bush and sea and sky.

In childhood it was visceral. I heard and smelled and felt and watched. I did not wonder or question, or need to explain the bliss of the natural world around me. Children's brains, though, develop into the questioning, abstract-thinking intelligences of teenagers. Phrases like *why*, and *what does it mean* began to intrude into the guilelessness of my childhood thinking.

And so the metaphysical hungers that accompany adolescence enticed me back to the anchorage of the church. The ability to think about life abstractly, the longing for a framework of meaning, lured me to enrol for preparation classes for Confirmation.

My parents were happy. Social outlets for teenagers were few in small-town Blenheim. Bible Class was one that seemed harmless. Other potential distractions such as hanging out in the only coffee bar in town, and kissing boys from the Air Force station up the road, embodied their fears for my virtue and safety.

I was desperate to make sense of the questions that invaded my transforming mind, so my teenage self consumed all that the Presbyterian Minister leading us had to offer.

He responded to all the questions I asked, as if he had not heard them before.

'Mr Robson, why would God hear what I say to him when there are millions of people praying?'

'Mr Robson, why does God let all those people in Africa starve and die?'

The Reverend Robson had three daughters, little money, a gentle voice, and a ruddy face. The last was a symptom of a heart that failed him when he was fifty-six. A small, disloyal part of me wanted to be one of his daughters. He was my anchor in the messy seas of adolescence in small-town New Zealand.

With his guidance, I sought God. I prayed, every night. I was an assiduous acolyte, and I read the Bible systematically. Nana Davis had given me one with a black embossed cover. I loved the fragile paper inside those covers, paper that rustled quietly when my fingers caressed it. I kept notes, followed instructions for extracting slivers of wisdom from its tissued pages. I went to church every Sunday, rejecting my parents' pleas to go to the bach at weekends. The search for God was imperative, but He held Himself aloof. He was coy in the face of my pleas to make Himself manifest. Lack of evidence was not, though, a deterrent - I needed too strongly to believe. In the absence of direct communication, I began to seek proof of His existence in the nature I had loved until now without reflection. I sat on a rock, discovered the metaphor of the sea/His love washing over everything, cleansing, omnipresent, clichéd. I was compelled by my insistent need to trust, to find faith, to find answers to my interrogations.

A collateral advantage to Bible Class was the social life. Its hygienic fun met the needs for adolescent intermingling – though not of limbs. The church held regular Bible Class dances, attended by teenagers from most of the respectable families in the town whether or not they came to church. We all knew how to dance – we had been taught by the maths teacher at our school, which, apart from a small convent, was the only High School in the town. Mr McClatchy was a small, bald, bespectacled mathematician who broke free from his algebraic demeanour every Tuesday after school to teach us the moves for waltzing, Gay Gordons, and two-steps. The transformation was bewildering. In class he moved gently, concentrated on focusing our wandering brains on solving equations. His patience was impressive. On the dance floor in the school hall his movements were fluid, energetic, his glasses discarded as he propelled one girl after another around the room, demonstrating guidance and gallantry to adolescent boys.

Our learning was tested within the suitable confines of school dances. Girls wore taffeta dresses and a little makeup, lipstick outlining anxious lips. Boys crammed their bodies into long trousers and shirts, wrists and ankles sprinkled with dark hairs, sweating their embarrassment. Girls lined up on one side of the hall, hoping to be picked by one of the less lumpy boys for the next dance. The coolest boys moved in a mini-herd across the hall, aiming for the three prettiest girls. We wallflower maidens were left with the dregs of the boys – either the clumsiest farm boys or, in my case, the most nerdy. Paul J was the son of one of our teachers. He was bespectacled and unpopular and I found myself twirling the floor with him. His hand was sticky around mine; it clasped it as if he feared falling if he let it go. In my ear his breaking voice croaked, 'Do you remember the formula Mr McClatchy taught us today?' No. So he recounted it, in detail, with an elegant ending ('Therefore, x equals nought') that coincided with the finish of the music for that dance.

There was no alcohol at these dances, school or Bible Class. No-one hid beer in the bushes out the back of the hall. We did not feel virtuous and nor did we consider ourselves deprived by our mini-culture of abstinence. Dancing enabled seemly physical contact without inflaming inadmissible lust. Kissing came much later.

Thirteen

At seventeen I left home to go and live in the United States for a year as an American Field Service student. In 1963, international air travel was cumbersome compared with today. Few people did it, and seats were uncomfortable. I was familiar with short flights in small planes from my childhood; this was something entirely different. There were no direct flights to the US from New Zealand, and the legs between countries were long. We flew from Auckland to Sydney, disembarked there, and boarded another plane to Hawaii. We were a cargo of excited and nervous child-adults, all strangers to each other, on a great adventure. By the time the third leg of the trip ended, the impact of landing at Los Angeles airport was muted by our developing familiarity with unfamiliarity, and with exhaustion from travelling.

I took with me a steadfast devotion to my pursuit of God. Everyone in the United States believed in God; you could not be the President if you were not a Christian. Religiosity was in handshakes, at mealtimes, on television, in school - unquestioned and, it began to seem to me, unexamined.

I went to church every Sunday with my host family. And dismayingly, the performance of religious observance started to seem rote. People prayed and sang in the local Lutheran Church as if they were cleaning their teeth while thinking of something else. No discussion, no questioning – just enactment of jaded ceremony.

There was, too, another disjunction. The parents in my host family were self-righteous in their church attendance and assertions about being good Christians. Their behaviour, though, began to seem bizarre. The father started to take a discomforting interest in me. He suggested that I change my hairstyle, and part it in the middle. The first inklings of indignation began to stir – I wrote in my diary: "It's my hair, I want it as it is." Still, the pious and shy country girl was eager to please. On my second day with the family the mother, with no warning, lifted her blouse up to her neck and displayed a hysterectomy scar, a red and angry snake stretching down her belly. I stared, then looked at her face. I had no idea what reaction she wanted, nor how to hide the melange of horror and fascination I felt. She was smiling, a smug curl at the edges of her mouth.

I began to make some friends at the High School. One of them, Cherry, invited me to go horse-riding. I was excited. I had given up the horse I had at home with reluctance, and an adolescent-girl obsession with horses still lingered. I asked my American family, who seemed alarmed that I was proposing to go somewhere with other people. The father demanded details of where, with whom, and especially of when. What time would the riding start? How long would we ride? Most importantly, what time would I be home? They knew Cherry's family; nonetheless, it was grudgingly that they gave me permission to go.

Cherry's mother picked me up and we went to the horse-riding centre and saddled up our horses with American saddles – high pommels, strange foot-encompassing stirrups. It felt blissful to be on a horse again. We rode a few minutes longer than planned, and we loitered to unsaddle, groom, and talk to the horses. I pushed my nose into the sweaty coat of the bay mare I had been riding – her smell transported me back to days of riding my horse up rivers in Blenheim on Saturdays with a friend and a packed lunch.

Cherry's mother collected us and returned me to the family twenty minutes after I had said I would be back. The father was waiting at the front door, hands on his hips, his face scrunched, his eyebrows drawn together over his eyes.

'Go to your room!'

I had never been sent to my room before. He offered no explanation. I went up the stairs. I waited, worried and bewildered. No sound from downstairs. I started a letter to my parents in New Zealand, telling them what had happened. An hour later, the father came into the room and asked me to confess. To what? That I had lied, I had not gone horse-riding, I had instead gone to Milwaukee to a coffee bar (the term spat out as one might say brothel), and drunk coffee.

I denied it. My words sounded unconvincing to me, and clearly to him as he stood there red and shaking. I did not give him the confession he was demanding; I had just that much strength of mind. Nonetheless, he told me in the voice of a preacher that he would forgive me. I swallowed my outrage, still in the business of pleasing.

Later, after a muted evening meal during which the other members of the family were silent, he told me to sit on the floor in the sitting room with the garish furniture, with my head between his knees. He was going to give me a neck massage. My sense of all this being wrong was swamped by my powerlessness, my inability to refuse. What would he have done to me if I had leapt up and run from the room? And where would I go? He wrenched my neck and I turned my face as far as I could from his crotch. I endured what he assured me was good for me.

Nothing worse happened, though it might if I had stayed in that household. I ended the letter to my parents with assurances that all was well – I feared that if I complained I would have to leave the school and the friends I had made. They ignored my reassurances and alerted the American Field Service authorities. A week later, in Earth Sciences class, I heard my name called over the school intercom. This was a weird arrangement through which the whole school could hear who was being summonsed, often for reprimand. I went to the principal's office, where the local head of American Field Service was waiting. She told me I could not go back to the family house, that she would collect all my belongings and take them to the new family I was to live with for the rest of my stay. The year after I left the United States, the vengeful father was jailed for fraud. And God did not save the mother; she was admitted to a psychiatric hospital.

Something was not right with their faith.

* * *

Back in Blenheim a year later, the Bible Class was waiting to embrace me for reasons other than welcoming a sister back to the fold. I had, they imagined, a whiff of exoticism, a smell of glamorous experience in that exciting country the US of A, which incited their curiosity. The focus was not on any spiritual enlightenment I might have acquired; rather, it was my anticipated ability to dance as they supposed the Americans did. At the first Bible Class social after I returned, all eyes were on my body – a body that had expanded on a diet of American milkshakes and S'mores. A S'more is a construction made of foods that on their own might be considered sinful. Two (at least) marshmallows are toasted and squashed between two Graham Crackers - sweet biscuits that are ubiquitous and much loved in the United States. The iniquitous but delicious sandwich is sometimes gilded by dipping the concoction in melted chocolate before eating it, increasing both the pleasure and the mess.

Dozens of sets of eyes watched as one of the older boys stepped over and took me onto the dance floor. A Beatles song was booming from the speakers. My stomach was pitching, my legs were leaden, my hips were frozen. I had done no dancing at all in the USA. I wanted very badly to sit down. And pretending exotic moves was not an option – I had no imagination to sustain that.

No brave new dance moves, no swivelling hips; eyes in disappointed faces turned elsewhere.

* * *

From my perspective on our current relationship, God and I had reached an equilibrium, a stable if unsatisfactory state. He continued to elude my immediate reality and I stayed constant in my attention to scripture and daily prayers. Stability, though, when it is uneven, rarely endures. And forces were afoot ready to sabotage our tenuous liaison.

Science was the first to strike. I went to university with limpid aspirations. Take sciences, the Careers Adviser said. You did well in biology in your last school year. And so I studied chemistry, mathematics, botany and zoology at Canterbury University. I looked for the hand of God, and found it absent in all I read and heard. The clean logic of scientific thinking began to nibble away at the edges of my beliefs.

The second demon doubt magnified my realisation in the United States that professing faith was not always accompanied by behaviour that matched the protestations. It came from the demeanour of fellow worshippers at the well-mannered Presbyterian Church I attended in suburban

Christchurch. No-one in the congregation seemed concerned about the Big Questions that still bothered me. Appearance and social intercourse, seen through the lens of my growing scepticism, seemed to be stronger motives for Sunday service attendance. Style seemed to be trumping substance. I smelled hypocrisy in the perfume of women and the aftershave of men, which matched the rote worshipping in the United States. My commitment to church was becoming shaky, and God still showed no initiative in maintaining our relationship.

I had started writing poetry, and I charted the beginnings of doubt at the age of nineteen in an earnest, overwrought poem.

The doctrine speaks
embodied in statues
embalmed in icons
fashioned in words of fear.

I kneel, cowed before the need for belief
humble beneath the scowl of elders,
crushed by the weight of tradition,
afraid.

A small voice speaks.
It tells of other beliefs,
other ways of knowing, unfettered
by darkness, uncowed by Hell.

I listen at night, but daybreak
hushes the voice. Prayers
silence the light. I
kneel, in obedience to
the inevitability of Right.

The corrosiveness of doubt was joined by something else. The yearning for intellectual nurturance, a thirst that had been assuaged in adolescence by the charismatic Presbyterian minister, was now increasingly met by the beguiling rigour of academic knowledge. In the third year of a science degree I added Philosophy 101 to the medley of science subjects. Plato, Socrates, Russell and Locke picked away at my fraying focus on a Christian God. Our one-way relationship began to unravel, and in the next two years God and I underwent an indeterminate, gentle separation. He did not protest. We drifted apart, with no apparent regrets on either side. I no longer went to church, and neither did I pray. I felt no loss.

* * *

Over the next nine years I drifted through agnosticism and toward frank disbelief. It was not at the start a total rejection of faith. It took the commonplace trajectory from the belief in God as interested in me as an individual, to acknowledgement of some vague kind of force beyond our knowing, and on to scepticism about even that possibility.

Ten years later, I took a graduate paper in philosophy of science, taught by the former priest who had deduced that I was pregnant. He retained an amiable air of reverence for life and of amusement with the world and himself. My first essay, its deduction embedded in philosophical turns of phrase, reasoned that the concept of God arises from the enterprise of humans envisaging the very finest that a person can be, and reifying that image. The essay coalesced all the thoughts, feelings, and provisional conclusions that had burbled away in my mind for the last decade. It made sense of my experiences. Generously, the ex-priest awarded it an A; I soon discovered that Humanists had beaten me to this conclusion many decades ago. The exercise of writing that essay, though, anchored and articulated my conclusions about religious belief, releasing any lingering faith in sentient forces beyond ourselves.

* * *

Alexander's dying might have brought about a reconciliation between God and me. I had been shameless in calling on Him and anyone else who might listen when Alexander was on life support. I do not see it as a virtue *not* to believe, *not* to have faith in God or some other form of encompassing being. It is simply the way my experiences have led and my conclusions have gone, ending in this hard place which is genuine for me, but not for many, many others. I was wistful, I was even envious, but I was not tempted. I am left with what the writer Geoff Dyer calls a god-shaped vacuum, a hollow that is both comfortable and a legacy of the path taken to what I believed then, and do today.

Instead of taking solace from the inscrutable intentions of a higher power, I have responded to Alexander's loss by rejecting conclusively the existence of such a being, who might somehow be the cause of my child dying or at least have not intervened to prevent his death. The conclusions of my philosophical essay were not challenged by his dying.

I came face-to-face with Alexander's death without the facility to even hope he might be in a better place, with no assurance that there was religious or cosmic meaning in his dying, or that someone larger and wiser than me held some enigmatic understanding. I am not a card-carrying atheist. I simply have no belief, no faith in a God or gods. All I had when Alexander died was a sense of authenticity in the place at which I had arrived, my knowing that this was tough but that it was right to hold fast to my unbelief. I had that, and the love of husband and family, to carry me through the next phase of life – a life without my baby.

Fourteen

It felt as if his death was not true, was a cruel dream. So long as my breasts ached and spurted and held milk, it seemed just possible that Alexander might return. It was, after all, his milk, they were his breasts. As the breast milk surged and receded and surged, so too did the hope. The delusion disappeared with the last of my milk.   Diary, June 1981

Back in the village, life resumed a way of being, wrapping itself around the absence that was a constant presence. Its darkness glowered inside and beside me, shadowing all I did. Outwardly, much was the same as before. Simon and Emily went to school each morning, clambering onto the school bus with the other children from the village. Jim went back to work at the medical centre. I had nowhere in particular to go, nothing much to do. Lilacs finished blooming and roses took their place, the blackbird sang its song from the top of the elm tree. The village was bewildered. The New Zealand family with the smiley baby had disappeared for five days and come back depleted.

I blamed myself for his death. A sting in the soggy mess of sadness was the possibility that I might have done something to prevent him dying. I lay in a bath until the water chilled, and I re-lived that Friday afternoon second by second, re-arranged it, made things happen differently. In my re-living I went upstairs earlier and I picked him up while he was wriggling, half awake. He woke, he smiled, and he lived. I did not give him yoghurt before he went to sleep. In my re-living I knew that an allergic reaction to cows' milk was one theory about the cause of Sudden Infant Death. I *knew* about SIDS. And I went back to Paris, where he had been sick two weeks earlier. We did not take him to the Bois de Bologne, where the cold air cut into his lungs and mine.

In my re-living I was a more vigilant mother; a better, more responsible mother.

And I blamed others. The ambulance driver could have gone faster. The anaesthetist in the ambulance could have tried harder, could have been more skilled, could have kept him breathing. He should have saved my baby's life. My sister Vellyn should have brought him around to consciousness, not just to breathing again. Blame, recrimination, rage and tears – these were my companions in those early weeks that followed his funeral and our journey to Stiffkey. Blame had begun to eat up all my energy.

In my most irrational moments, I blamed Jim. My reptilian brain, the brute animal in me, lashed around, searching for explanation. It focused for a while on Jim's encouragement to take Alexander to the Bois de Bologne as he was recovering from his sickness in Paris, Jim's reassurance that it would be safe to do so. Taking him out did not cause him to die. But this illogical nugget of possibility mutated like a cancer cell, grew and invaded my rational self. Even in the impotence of grief, I knew it was wrong and deeply unfair to blame Jim. I had agreed with him, we had taken Alexander together. I was not able to tell him about those feelings then; maybe some honesty at that time might have kept us on a constructive trajectory.

The realisation that blame was both misplaced and destructive was slow to come. We act, in the moment, as best we can. All of us did – the anaesthetist did his best in the ambulance, Vellyn was heroic in her efforts to revive him. Forgiveness of myself and of Jim and of others seeped in over the weeks to quiet my rants against myself, fate, and other people. And alongside forgiveness, a slow-rising understanding and acceptance that blame was corrosive began to emerge. No-one, nothing, was to blame. Alexander's death was not under anyone's control. Yet in that realisation was embedded a road spike – there was *no reason* why he died. No-one to blame, so no explanation. I felt like a boat with no steerage, swinging in the wind with no idea where it should be facing. The understanding that blame was pointless brought with it both a sense of calm and a feeling of floundering. Our need to explain things that happen to us is fundamental to being human - and there was no explanation for his death.

* * *

In those days after the funeral I moved slowly through the spaces of the house, through the hours of each day, staying inside to avoid the abrasion of meeting and talking to other people. I had bleeding surfaces to protect. Hiding away is a time-limited activity, however, and I found myself having to face the reactions of people in our village and in shops. At first, seeing them felt as if sandpaper was being dragged across my wounds. I recoiled from the blast of people's clumsy sympathy.

We had a neighbour, an Anglo-Indian whose glorious wife was killed in a car accident about the same time that Alexander was born. Jagdeesh was a gentle man whose demeanour made even English formality seem rough. He was infused with calm despite all that he had endured. Two weeks after Alexander's death, I had a dream. Jagdeesh came to our front door carrying a shoebox. In it was a miniature Alexander. He told me he'd found him on the road and was returning him. Alexander was wizened and dried; I was hopeful and distraught, all jumbled up in the dream.

It was impossible to leave the village without passing the home of Sarah, my friend with the baby girl the same age as Alexander. In those first days I looked to the left as I drove past, staring into someone else's front yard in case Sarah was in hers. I dreaded seeing her more than I wanted to avoid anyone else. I did not know what I would say. I feared what *she* would say, and I guessed how she might be feeling. The time came when we could no longer avoid each other. Her mouth said the expected, the proper words – *How are you? So sorry.* Her whole being radiated fear – fear of contamination, of the death of my baby somehow leaching out to infect hers.

Her body moved to protect her daughter, to screen her from me and me from her. Words of comfort found their way to my lips. Don't worry, Sarah. It won't happen to you. Neither of us was convinced.

My heart was far too chaotic for me to appreciate the fear felt by other parents. Sarah's reaction was typical of several mothers whom I met in those first weeks. They shuffled physically and verbally, they avoided me if it was possible. If we did meet, their eyes dodged mine and they shunned the topic of Alexander. They did not know what to do. They didn't know what to say. I had no idea what I needed them to say or do. Their silence was wounding, their avoidance felt cowardly.

In *Levels of Life*[3], Julian Barnes, the English novelist, quotes the words of a poet friend whose wife had died:

but I too have met the tribal will to impose
taboos and codes, and have behaved rudely,
invoking my dead wife in dinner table conversation.
A beat of silence, of shared fear and sick shock, falls.

Christopher Reid (p. 72)

Barnes talks, too, of the time, soon after his wife's death, when he had a meal with three friends who had known her well. He says:

---

[3] *Levels of Life*. Julian Barnes, 2013. Jonathan Cape, London.

I mentioned her name; no-one picked it up. I did it again, and again nothing. Perhaps the third time I was deliberately trying to provoke, being pissed off at what struck me not as good manners but cowardice. Afraid to touch her name, they denied her thrice, and I thought the worse of them for it.

(p. 73)

Acknowledgement of the life and death of Alexander was what I needed. I wanted his life affirmed, not denied. But I did not know that then.

* * *

Something else was painful to me at that time. Platitudes. And some were not just anaemic, they were offensive.

'It was meant to be.'

These words were particularly distressing. What did they mean? That someone, something, God maybe, *decreed* that our baby should die? Some being had to mean it to be, so it assumed a sentient force outside ourselves. The implication was that Alexander's death had happened for some greater purpose – that somehow it was intended, that it was a sacrifice demanded of us in order that something else, presumably something more worthy, might happen.

I doubt that those who use this phrase think about what "it was meant to be" is really saying. Its implication, when the meaning of the words is examined, is that one's loss is in the hands of a higher being or force, that there is no reason to grieve and indeed no cause for grief. That our loss is insignificant in the light of the greater good that (one presumes) will eventuate. Like most attempts at comfort, these words are offered with no intention of hurting or offending the bereaved. And like so many efforts to console a person for whom comfort is not possible given what has happened, "it was meant to be" can also be a self-soothing phrase.

It is meant well; but it was deeply repugnant - at least to me. Perhaps I was too sensitive.

* * *

Our next-door neighbour in Bygrave was Graham. He had retired as an electrician and followed his real passion, being the village know-everything-you'd-ever-need-to-know person, and supplier of bargains from his back shed. From there, like a grotesque miracle, he had produced for us an enormous turkey at Christmas time – wholesale, of course. I had tried to imagine the bird on its feet, and concluded that it had never strutted. No bird's legs could have supported such a body.

Graham, who himself was beginning to resemble a Christmas turkey, came to the door. His body shouted embarrassment. 'I'm so sorry your baby died,' he said. 'I *know* how you feel. My cat died last month.' He sweated his sympathy on the doorstep.

A colleague of Jim's, a senior physician in the hospital, wrote a letter. It went something like this:

Dear Jan and Jim

Please don't worry about your baby. He is safe in heaven with God and he has puppies to play with. Our dog had puppies a few weeks ago and they died.

Best wishes

Mark and Susan

I wanted to light his letter and put the burning paper under his sanctimonious face, catch his hair alight, incinerate the smugness out of him.

People offered other consolations.

'You'll get over this. It might not feel like it right now.'

'Have another baby soon – you'll get over him more quickly that way.'

'You're lucky he was so young – it would be worse if he was older.'

Or they went on quickly to tell me at length about their aunt or their grandmother or their brother, and *their* gruelling experiences of losing a baby. I did not want to hear. This was *my* pain. Their eyes beseeched me not to talk about my situation, not to elaborate, above all not to show how my heart was leaking blood.

Some talked to me as if I was an imbecile. Their voices, their words, trod carefully around me, proceeded slowly as if I had difficulty understanding, as if I was somehow cognitively impaired.

* * *

I sat in the living room of our house in Wedon Way. Opposite me was Linley. She was a little younger than me, plump and crumpled and sad. She lived in the next village. I poured tea from the flowered teapot that belonged to the house, into wide, fragile matching tea cups.

Her daughter had died four weeks before. Unlike Alexander, but like most babies who die of SIDS, she was found cold and dead in the morning. She was not temporarily rescued on a sunny afternoon with an aunt around to perform resuscitation. Linley and I had been brought together by a local community worker, hoping we could share our sorrow and support each other.

We tried, Linley and me. We looked at each other's faces, gazed at each other's grief. We had no words to say to each other after the facts had been exchanged. We could not recognise our selves or our precise sadness in the other person.

We could not understand the ways in which the other was confronting the similar demons we separately experienced. There was no common ground, and we met only once.

We might have done it better had a third person been there to facilitate. And yet, I know I would have recoiled at such a contrived gathering. I had not thus far found a way to absorb support that would work for me.

* * *

Letchworth, where Jim worked, was becoming an increasing anathema. Shopping there meant exposure to depressed citizens and drab shops, and above all to memories of the alert little face who used to make it all seem okay. His indiscriminate grin, lighting his pale face beneath his arc of dark hair – so tempting to see that hair as a halo – lightened the faces of some of those unhappy fellow shoppers. I hadn't realised then that I was proud of him; proud of his beauty and liveliness and lovingness.

And I would see, in high fidelity, harassed women screaming at their babies. If only they would understand how precious they were; I wanted to shake them and say, 'Hold your baby, love him and want him.' Instead, I turned away, skulking under my sadness.

I took Alexander's photo – a negative – in to get enlarged, and was told by the woman in Boots the Chemist that it wasn't much good and I should take another photo of him.

'He's dead,' I told her.

She looked at my face, hers impassive. She grasped the negative with greasy fingers and took it off to discuss with someone out the back. When she returned I pointed out that she was still holding it with her fingers on it.

'I've worked here for seventeen years.' Her face was flushing. 'I know what I'm doing with negatives.'

She turned her body and looked back toward that mysterious private area shops have for their staff. When she turned back her eyes looked smaller.

'Anyway, I've lost people in my family, too.'

I left the shop. I was hurt, she was hurt, no-one won that exchange.

Three weeks after Alexander died, I went in to the medical centre where Jim worked. It was a familiar routine. Alexander and I had often called by to greet and be welcomed by receptionists, nurses and other doctors – and, when he had a moment, Jim. The centre was a one-storeyed character-free

1960s building, clean and boring. The nurses and receptionists hugged me, gathered around. How was I? One of Jim's medical partners came out to the reception area, and I felt his helplessness through the arms that briefly circled me.

In a cramped office up the grey-lighted hallway Jim was seeing patients, fixing their pain, sorting their problems, hurting inside.

'How do you think Jim is?' I asked. 'I know he hides it well, but he's pretty upset.'

They looked confused. No-one had an answer. Fathers, I realised, were assumed not to feel the pain of loss the way mothers do. They get on with their work and they get over it. It is a challenge to hug a man, especially a tall, strong man, who might embarrass himself by crying. I doubt they hugged Jim.

Fifteen

Julian Barnes tells of a few attempts at comfort that worked, like the friend who said to him at a gathering, 'There's someone missing.' Similarly, I found that some acts of condolence were positive, often in ways I could not predict and still do not understand. We had a friend, a Catholic paediatrician, who came from London late one Friday afternoon to visit us in the sunlit Bygrave house. Long, skinny wrists emerged from jacket sleeves that struggled to reach to the ends of his arms, his hair flew about his head like an electrified halo, and his shirt peered out from beneath the back of his coat, where he had forgotten to tuck it into his waistband. Gerard's relationships with the world were complicated. He wrestled with his faith, he argued with his profession, and he failed in his love affairs. He came into the living room and threw his long body in a heap on the sofa, his limbs wrapping around each other in improbable ways. His face wore his sorrow for us like a shroud. Sun played over the shadows on his face, exaggerating its hills and valleys. We poured him a whisky.

'I'm not going to pray for Alexander,' he said. 'I am going to ask my priest to pray for you.'

He spoke quietly, without guile or embarrassment. Somehow this felt apt, although then I did not know why. He was not pretending that Alexander was in heaven playing with puppies. He really believed that those of us left bereft just might be helped by priestly petitions. He was offering the best he could with no moral imperatives. We hugged him as he untangled his arms from his legs, unfurled himself from the sofa, and went out of the door to his car.

A week after the funeral, Barbara drove up from London, blooming in the last days of her pregnancy. She leaned forward a little as she walked, minimising the size of her bump. We went out into the garden that was burgeoning in the late spring and we dawdled down the path to the end by the fields, past rose bushes throwing their sensuous aromas at us. Muffin zigzagged in front, her nose glued to the trail of an animal by now well gone from the garden. Spikes of young wheat reached up to the sun in the field beyond the garden, smelling of youth, of green, of energy. Barbara was blossoming with a new life, I was stinging with the loss of one. We had no words, we'd said them all. We wept together for Alexander.

So much hurt, so much confusion, so little understanding. Those who offered us comfort face-to-face were as bewildered as I was. None of us knew what was right. For me there was no comfort given or taken that worked in those early days. I was grieving, beyond the reach of consolation. And had I been the person trying to offer me comfort, I would have been at a loss.

And what ultimately works for one person will not do for another. I was a person in mourning who was idiosyncratic – curmudgeonly, even - in what I found helpful.

I have learned, now, what worked for me in being offered consolation. First, and most enduringly – for it still matters, thirty-four years later – acknowledging the life and death of Alexander is foremost. Pretending he did not exist is a way of pretending he did not die. Perhaps it is easy to forget the existence of a baby who lived for just fifteen weeks; how much easier, then, it is to forget or ignore the existence of a baby who is stillborn, who dies at birth or even earlier through miscarriage. For this parent and, I suspect, for most, affirming a baby's life is sustaining. That means asking about the baby. What was she like? Tell me about her personality, what she looked like.

A second aspect of effective consolation is to listen rather than to talk. Bereaved parents need to talk about their baby or child, again and again and again. But we do not. Others are uncomfortable, they change the subject, shift their eyes to somewhere over our shoulder, so we stay silent in order to avoid their discomfort. Soliciting talk about the baby or child is profoundly nourishing.

For me, hugs were potent therapy. Often, wordless comfort can say what a person wants to convey far more effectively than clumsy words.

Offering practical help is also good. Babysitting? Supermarket shopping? Going for a walk or to a movie? Life goes on after a death, and distraction is sometimes exactly right.

I came to understand the fright of other parents. Their baby might die – mine did. And I might somehow make this happen by spreading the germ of death. Our otherwise ample capacity for compassion seems to disappear when we have to confront some terror that might in turn affect us.

And I understand, now, the perplexity that confounds the sympathetic intentions people have when wanting to offer consolation. Most of us have no idea what to say to someone who is hurting their way through the loss of a loved person. I found many times that what was said was hurtful, at least at the time. I was angry and affronted by the efforts of some whose sincerity was not in doubt. My emotions were too new, too unfamiliar, too unprocessed, to see the good intentions masked by a lack of knowing how to console bereaved parents.

Honesty, authenticity, physical comforting such as embraces, genuine sharing of grief, space and permission to feel what I was feeling – these were the things that worked for me.

* * *

Eleven days after Alexander died, I was in a hospital room at Queen Charlotte Hospital, in the antenatal ward. Simon and Emily were with me. It might have been the same room where

Alexander and I had started to recognise and to become besotted with each other. Barbara had just given birth to Jonathan; she lay in the bed I might have been in and he was in a cot beside her.

He was a facsimile of Alexander. He was perfect and, as many babies in our family do, he had dark hair and alabaster skin. Every bit of me had wanted to come here and meet him, for a muddle of reasons most of which I could not articulate. I did not know how it would be.

I was a jumble. My most unselfish, emotionally rational self was joyous that a new baby had joined our beloved family. My love for Barbara overrode any hesitation about greeting her son.

The emotionally irrational me was screaming, a cascade of disjointed messages. He might die! He's too perfect. It's not fair – why did *our* baby die? I want him.

As we walked out into the hospital car park, Simon's seven-year-old hand slid into mine.

'Mummy, Vellyn said Alexander wasn't going to die.'

As weeks went on I found that increasingly I needed to be by myself. Day-to-day stuff was calling on energies I did not have. I wanted to curl up with my hands over my face and sleep until some kind of will to move crept back into my limbs.

People – friends and family – made sure I was not alone. I appreciated their love, their thoughtfulness, but I needed space to miss Alexander. Being distracted from remembering what had happened made it so much worse when the reality was allowed to crash in.

Day-to-day life was back to normal. The funeral was over, the ashes were scattered, and there were four of us. We had been four for four-and-a-half years, and five for only fifteen weeks. Simon and Emily played with village friends after school, squabbled and adored each other. I was no longer crying in the shower.

But we were not normal. We were still in a state of grief. A constant undertow of sorrow and loss pulled at us in everything we did. It came with us on weekends away. It was in the bed, ready to flow into dreams and wakefulness at any moment. It tugged at snatches of music, transforming them into lancing memories that hurt again and again.

Sometimes it seemed as if Alexander might be upstairs, if I just went and looked. Or, if I thought about being at the local hospital hard enough, that the hope that we had clutched then that he would live might return, and time might reverse. Those self-deceptions soon faded; I began to wonder if that was what people meant by "getting over it".

Sixteen

Alexander is recorded in the British system as having died from SIDS, or cot death. SIDS is defined by the *absence* of a diagnosis, of a known cause for a baby's death. When an unexpected infant death occurs, post-mortems search infant bodies for clues about why they die, and they find nothing. Baby hearts are robust, their lungs and livers and kidneys are breathing and filtering and firing. Their blood is fine and so, seemingly, is their brain. The term SIDS is an inside-out diagnosis, an empty shell that tells us only what we don't know. It is a negative without a positive, a yin without a yang.

No virus or bacterium infected Alexander's infant tissues, and his death was not the result of an accident. Campaigns for better antibiotics or safer roads would not prevent a SIDS death. There is still no accounting for babies dying as Alexander did. It happens, quietly and quickly, and no-one can tell parents why.

* * *

Brains are deeply mysterious, grey, wrinkly, unpretty lumps of matter. We don't see a brain often. We don't feel its actions as we do a heartbeat. When it hurts we call it a headache, not a brainache. It is enclosed, out of reach, inside a bony box that protects it from the abrasions of everyday life. And so it is easy to ignore this powerhouse of our existence, the foundation of our wellbeing, the monitor and protector of our hearts and minds and bodies. Yet a brain is a miraculous, meticulous organ that starts blooming in the first weeks of our life as an embryo. It buds like a lotus at the top of the neural tube, the slice of tissue that folds around and joins its edges in the first heartbeat days. The neural tube closes on itself, resembling a piston, until one end expands and becomes an immensely complex knob. It is the genesis of our minds, our thoughts, our loves and our hates and our sadnesses, our loftiest ideas and our basest motives. When its function falters we are in mortal danger. We risk physical disabilities, derangement, hallucination and incomprehension. And if it fails to tell our bodies to keep breathing, we die.

The part of this miraculous organ that keeps our bodies breathing is in the brain stem. It is the lower part of the brain that connects to the spinal cord. In particular, it is the medulla oblongata – a name rigid with consonants - that in concert with the more prosaically named pons, makes sure that the muscles needed to breathe in and to breathe out are prompted to act. The medulla oblongata is the consistency and shape of a sausage. The medulla and the pons also ensure that we are aroused to wake if our oxygen supply is threatened. That tiny button-sized portion of our brain stem, the medulla oblongata, is responsible for our staying alive. In tandem with the pons, it keeps us breathing.

Most of the time, we do not think about our breathing. The medulla induces our bodies to inhale, exhale, breathe more quickly or more slowly as it decides that we need more or less oxygen. There are times, though, when we try to control our inhalations and exhalations. Singers exercise their breathing in order to maximise their voice production. Sports people develop control over their breathing in order to fuel the exertions they ask of their bodies; efforts that extend beyond those like me, who do not push ourselves physically. And yoga teachers seek to exert control over their breathing in order to attain changed states of mind.

In a less energetic way, we focus on our breathing when we want to be soothed, to lower stress. Inhalation, exhalation, mindfulness and meditation techniques encourage us to concentrate on this most fundamental activity of our bodies – an activity initiated and monitored by these awe-inspiring, unseen organs in our heads.

Babies practise breathing before they are born. Their chests move in and out, rehearsing the movements upon which their lives will depend when they emerge. At birth there is nothing playful about those movements. The medulla oblongata starts the work of overseeing the bringing-in and the pushing-out of air that is essential to being and staying alive. That piece of tissue, just one centimetre wide, kicks into action and keeps working flawlessly for fifty, seventy, ninety years.

Unless it fails. In babies who die of SIDS something goes wrong in their infant brain stem, and breathing stops. The baby brain falters at its base, stutters, and closes down its messages to lungs and muscles. And the medulla and the pons stay their message to wake up, to start breathing again. Silently, with no alarm beeps, the sleeping infant dies. This is why, like Linley's daughter, most often babies who have died from SIDS are found in the morning, lifeless, in their cots.

Nobody knows why this happens, yet.

In the time soon after Alexander's death, the need to explain to myself why he died led me to a place of tentative clarification. There seemed to be more than one factor involved – the piercing coincidence of his vulnerability to failing to breathe, with some kind of trigger outside his body. He had a potential in his tiny brain for failure of the systems fundamental to his living, and he happened to experience an environmental factor – the way he was sleeping, the temperature, perhaps – that led to the fatal coincidence of factors that caused him to die. This was the explanation I gave myself.

That hypothesis is still the best that can be proposed. There is still no understanding of what causes the pons and the medulla oblongata to falter. Nor is there an understanding about why some babies are vulnerable and others are not. There is, though, a much-advanced comprehension of the environmental risk factors associated with SIDS. The most dramatic is the sleep position of babies. Babies who sleep on their fronts have a greater chance of stopping breathing, and dying. In the UK, the risk of infants dying has been reduced by 70% through the message to parents to put babies to sleep on their backs. And this understanding is predominantly thanks to the research of a New Zealand researcher, Professor Ed Mitchell, whose careful examination of risk factors has led to the "back to sleep" movement throughout the world.

Two related factors have been found to increase the risk for SIDS. One is co-sleeping with infants – having the baby in bed with parents. Smoking near babies is also a risk factor. The evidence is strong and clear – putting babies to sleep on their backs, not having them sleep in the same bed as adults, and not smoking near babies, reduces the numbers of infants who die unexpectedly.

Yet these factors – sleep position, co-sleeping, smoking - are not *causes* of SIDS; babies sleep in all kinds of positions and do not die. Hundreds of thousands of babies slept on their tummies thirty years ago, and almost all of them did not die. The ones who did, who do, are made susceptible by the fragility of that sausage-shaped part of their brain.

A crucial distinction is that between risk and cause. Risks are things that are associated with the rate of infant death, but are not inevitable. A baby may have parents who smoke, but that baby will not necessarily die. The awareness of risk factors, and messages to parents that help reduce those risks, are imperative, and has lowered rates of SIDS worldwide. Yet there remains a core of deaths that are unexplained, and that are not prevented by lowering risk factors. We simply do not know what *causes* these deaths, although researchers think it is a combination of factors – that ill-fated coming together of vulnerability and trigger.

Another distinction that might well be emphasised to young parents being given information about SIDS is that between *unexpected* and *unexplained*. The majority (although not all) of infant deaths are unexpected. Unless a baby has an obvious illness from which it will die, we expect our infants to live.

Over half of unexpected deaths in the UK, after post-mortem examination, are also unexplained. In New Zealand, a little less than half are found to be unexplained. Explanations when found include infection, strangulation, and suffocation.

About a half of unexpected infant deaths cannot yet be explained.

The failure to make these distinctions clear runs the risk of engendering parental blame and guilt. The International Society for the Study and Prevention of Perinatal and Infant Death (ISPID) has recently cautioned against vilifying parents of babies who die. In New Zealand the term used most frequently is SUDI – Sudden Unexpected Death in Infancy. Although this includes both explained and unexplained deaths, the importance of the distinction is not always evident to anxious parents, nor to those who are grieving the death of their child. Advice to parents is sometimes worded as 'preventing SUDI', despite the fact that a half of unexpected deaths are also unexplained deaths. They cannot be prevented, given the lack of understanding to date.

I felt guilty, I blamed myself and others when Alexander died. If he had died today, guilt and blame might have been many times more intense, because I would have been told that it could have been prevented. Somehow, we need a double message to go out to parents – do all you can to reduce risk factors, and although you will never know you have done it, you may prevent your baby from dying. But, there is also a chance if your baby dies unexpectedly that there was nothing you could have done to prevent it. It is a delicate balance.

And although parents of babies who die from unexplained causes almost always blame themselves as they grieve, I found some comfort in the nebulous knowledge that there are many, many times when parents *prevent* their children from dying. Day-to-day care and ordinary vigilance ensure that babies are, in the overwhelming majority of cases, kept safe. We do not know how often or when an action saves a baby's life but it is logical to assume that it does, over and over. We perform unrecognised acts of omission or commission that save lives as a matter of everyday love and care.

Alexander's death was unexpected and unexplained. No-one's fault. Not preventable. If only I had known.

Seventeen

What might my child have become had he not died? The life he lived was excruciatingly short. His potential life, perhaps eighty or ninety years, is forever a mystery.

Some months ago when a friend's ninety-three-year-old father, a composer, died, 500 people gathered to honour the end of a lived life – not just a long life but a span that was fully inhabited. His personality and his achievements were celebrated, and there was some sadness that he was no longer living that rich and full life.

No-one thought much about his potential life, the one he had yet to lead. He might have composed another song cycle. But at ninety-three the possibilities for growth and generativity were all but exhausted. Had he lived on, his life would have continued to diminish as his faculties frayed and failed him. More celebration than mourning, then.

When Alexander died, we grieved the tiny proportion of his life that was lived. There were a few clues to grasp about him -

his easy-going personality and his joy in living, for example. His potential life, though, could only be imagined.

It was this unknowable future that we mourned, alongside the grieving for the loss of the baby we had known for fifteen weeks. We were mourning a chimera, a fantasy that had few boundaries.

Most parents have hopes for their children. For some these are drawn in detail. *She will go to university. He will be a better sportsman than his father. He will be taller than me.* For others, their aspirations are generalised and worthy hopes that, for example, their baby will become a happy and kind adult.

Our aspirations for Alexander were of a different, fuzzy variety – they were embryonic and unformed. We rejoiced, simply, in his babyness. We loved him profusely by the day, and assumed that his tomorrows would happen. Now he is frozen in time as a fifteen-week-old baby.

It is easy to imagine, given his baby joyousness, that he would have been an enchanting toddler, a sweet schoolboy, a happy child loved and teased by his older sister and brother.

Speculation becomes more diffuse when I imagine his teenage self. The exquisite agonies of limbs out of control, nose too big for his face, and torments of hormones, would have been standard issue. Acne might have smitten him, mottling his skin and bumping up against his fragile teen-boy self-image. He might have resorted to that fall-back vocalising of so many interminably embarrassed teenagers, grunting to cover the spikes and valleys of his breaking voice dancing up and down out of his control.

I think of how he would be now, grown up. He would be tall – lankiness is in his genes. He would almost certainly be a brown-eyed, dark-haired, light-skinned man, since he was a brown-eyed, dark-haired, light-skinned baby. His older brother is tall, auburn-haired, light-skinned, glorious; his older and younger sisters are dark-haired, tall and glorious. It is hard to imagine that he would not be glorious. But maybe not.

Imagining him physically is the easy part.

He would have grown up immersed in a middle class mini-culture that assumed he would go to university. Perhaps he would have rebelled, left school and home early, taken his twenty-first century version of a knapsack and pursued his questions and dreams in less conventional ways.

He might have taken drugs that addled his brain. He might have fathered a child at seventeen, or fifteen. He might have gone to prison, he might have been autistic. He might have been an artist, a musician, a writer, an actor.

He will be none of these things. All his possible futures, his potential lives, died with him, were closed in that small, white coffin.

But I can't help wondering.

***

We don't expect our babies to die, especially first-world babies. The huge majority – 99.8% - of infants in western countries do not die. Even in 1980s England, less than one baby in every thousand born died of SIDS, and the rate has halved now.

To put that into perspective, if a neonatal ward had thirty babies in the nursery, one baby in thirty-three nurseries would have died of SIDS. Or, one in thirty-three school classrooms would be missing a child because they had died of SIDS.

In 1981, some factors were under suspicion as possible risks. They included being a boy; having a mother who smoked in pregnancy; having a mother who smoked around the baby; being premature; being low birth weight; not being breastfed. Alexander was a boy. All the other factors did not apply to him. One out of six.

Jim and I did not think about the risk of SIDS – it did not cross our minds. We had two healthy children, no-one we knew had experienced the death of their baby, or known anyone who had. It simply was not contemplated. Had we thought about it, quite rationally we would have expected our baby to live.

It was a gruesome lottery, and our number came up. His death was unexpected, untimely, and unexplained.

A century or so ago, parents might have gazed on their newborn, knowing that there was a fifty-fifty chance that she would not live beyond early childhood. In Europe, just over half of babies survived until the age of five. Even fewer would reach adulthood.

Knowing the odds, perhaps they held themselves back from falling in love with their babies. Avoiding building a close connection with a child who had a good chance of dying would be self-protective and for many this would not be the first baby at risk. A letter written in the early 19th century illustrates the losses that were typical then:

My sister Polly who is nam^d for you mam, is married to a Doctor as worthy a man as now lives – in a partner She is one of the happiest of women But of the Bitter Cup of affliction She has Drank often & in Large Draughts She has been the Mother of four Smiling Babes But is Deprived of all by that hand that has an undoubted right to take when he pleases She Lost 3 in 17 Days 1 aged 3 years one 17 months one of 1 month & in a year another of 3 weeks – But She with her Companion Say the Lord Gave and taketh I believe they are Carefull to add Blessed be his name Such patterns of resignation were you to See them you wou^d think was not often to be found[4]

---

[4] From *Memorio of Mary Wilder White*. 1903 Elizabeth Amelia Dwight. Ed. Mary Wilder Tyleson.

Historians bicker about whether or not mothers in the 18th century loved their infants as freely as they do now. Most assume that there is little difference. There are few records of how parents felt about losing their infants in the 18th and 19th centuries since many people did not write. However, given the overwhelming falling-in-love that mothers and fathers experience for neonates, it is hard to imagine parents two centuries ago being able to hold back their love just in case their baby did not survive.

In the confidence that infants will not die today's parents interleave their lives with their babies' before they are born. Even before conception they are encouraged to prepare for their beginnings by taking dietary supplements. Scans ensure that they can know the baby's sex, they follow their growth, they watch their eyes blinking and their hands wringing. Apps for smartphones tell them how long their babies are and what they are doing on a given day. It is almost impossible not to form a relationship with these tiny heartbeating beings. The link parents form with an unborn baby is more than physical; it is emotional, and personal, often to the extent that the baby is named in advance of face-to-face meeting. And this enables fathers to engage with their infants before they are born – something more difficult to do before it was possible for scans and tests to peer inside the female enclosure that held the baby's secrets.

Birth, then, becomes a joyful encountering with a person parents feel they already know. Mothers put their newborns to their breasts, feed them within minutes of birth. Fathers, and often siblings, are there to meet and hold. To be entranced and engaged with newborns is both expected and commonplace.

No surprises, then, that parents are traumatised when a baby or a child dies. It is rare and unexpected, and happens despite all the precautions they have been exhorted to take. They know them, have seen them, fallen in love with them, before they are born; there is no holding back. Based on the odds, they let themselves become irretrievably besotted.

The technology of pregnancy and childbirth reassures us that our babies will live.

Eighteen

For Simon and Emily, Alexander was a singing baby brother who posed no threat to either of them. He did not usurp Emily's position as the baby of the family. She was not a baby and she knew it. He was not a rival for Simon's rank as oldest son. He was a benign baby who laughed when they tickled him, whose face lit up when they sang to him. He was a presence, a focus, a playmate, a joy. And then he died.

He was a strand woven through their lives for just fifteen weeks. His dying deprived them of a source of delight that they woke to daily in those weeks. They were bereft, they were confused, and our arms went around them to comfort and protect. The need to hold them through their child grief rose up through our self-soothing impulses, to take precedence. We, their mother and father, were focused on them, although our resources felt depleted and inadequate.

Our anguish was perhaps as distressing for them as their loss of Alexander. We were frequently distracted and distanced and we had no idea how to soothe them. Our seven-year-old son and our five-year-old daughter were living day-to-day with an appalling event, and with parents who succeeded only partially in supporting them. They were sad, we were sadder. In two days our demeanour had transformed from pervasive happiness to numbing distress.

Simon was overtly despondent. At seven he expressed his grief with gentleness, sitting on our knees and hugging us close. He was sufficiently old to understand the finality of Alexander's death, to know he would not return. Emily, aged five, was confused. For her, at five years old, death was not necessarily permanent. She was puzzled by our sadness. She found me weeping in the shower a few weeks after Alexander died.

'Why are you crying, Mummy?'

I wonder what they said to their friends. How does a child explain the death of a baby to someone of their age? Perhaps nothing was said to or by other children – perhaps playground action went on as before, loss unacknowledged. I knew that at their age their world was one of concrete things and actions. Alexander's death was an event, one that we could describe, although explanation was beyond us. So their few 'why' questions went unanswered.

Children of the age Simon and Emily were then see their world in egocentric ways. They are the centre of it, they are all-powerful in a way that can overwhelm them. This means that they are prone to blaming themselves for things that happen, including deaths.

Emily climbed on to my knee a few months later.

'Mummy, would Alex have been all right if we hadn't wanted peanut butter sandwiches after school?'

The concept of death itself is bewildering for children. Because they do not understand that it is permanent, it is possible in their minds that the dead person might come alive again. Bodies may still be able to feel things – how terrifying, then, to imagine a person being cremated. They need to be told and retold and helped to understand that being dead is not the same as being asleep. In her book about children's grief, Pam Heaney tells the story of an eight-year-old girl whose response to the loss of her grandmother was not just sadness, but fear.[5] Heaney, by asking the right questions, enabled her to voice her belief that her Nanna would feel it when the fire burned – she was being cremated.

We did not know this. Simon and Emily did not see Alexander's body. Did we explain cremation to them? Probably, but also probably inadequately. Emily's understanding of the mechanics of it failed her when she expected the coffin to come out of the crematorium chimney.

Current opinion varies as to whether or not children should see a dead body of someone they love. I believe that Emily and Simon were too young to cope with the contradictions of

---

[5] Heaney, Pam. *Children's Grief. A Guide for Parents*. Longacre Press 2004.

seeing the body of their brother but not fully understanding the concept of death. Older children can be prepared with careful explanation for seeing a body; as with so many other aspects of children, there are individual differences and it is a difficult decision that needs to be made on a case-by-case basis.

The language of young children is not adequate to the expression of their feelings. Were we sufficiently sensitive to this to help them to articulate what they were feeling? I hope we were. We did not try to hide our grown-up sadness from them, we encouraged them to talk about their feelings.

What Simon and Emily needed – as most children need when they and their family are grieving – were responses that matched their emotional and cognitive levels of development.

They needed to know *what* had happened, and why. We could not answer the second.

They needed reassurance – that what happened was not their fault, that they were loved and safe, that they and we would be all right.

They needed stability – for their world to stay as close to what they knew as possible.

They needed us to listen and to hear their fears and worries and questions.

They needed us to be strong, if not at the time then soon.

* * *

Our adult memories of when we were five or seven are like dreams. We can recall slivers, splotches, highlights, often vividly. And what we remember is seemingly random. At the age of five, when I started school, I remember paying a penny for hot cocoa in the winter; I remember being the worst artist in the infant class. I do not have a unified picture of being five, of what was happening at home, of other details of school. We may remember our school lunches, we might recall catching a bus, we will remember the morning we were bullied on the way to school. But we do not have a complete recollection of that time of our lives. The patches do not join up to a coherent scenario of what happened then. And, confusingly, we recall events and objects that do not seem to have any particular significance from our adult vantage. Neither Simon nor Emily as adults has memories of specific events in that April of 1981. Instead, they recall the emotions, the encompassing sadness of Jim and me.

Most of all when I think of how Alexander fits into the past I think of you and Dad. And how absolutely devastating and awful and sad it was for you both... When I do think back I have the impression you were quite sad a lot of the time. I sometimes think about how long the melancholy affected you for, during the years and years that followed. Simon, 2014

We *were* melancholy, far more than we realised. We functioned at a practical level, doing what had to be done. For them and for us, life had to go on, and it did. They continued going to school, we all went to Germany for a holiday in our VW camper van. They squabbled in the back, we yelled at them. The bass notes of Alexander's death rumbled quietly under the rhythms of our ongoing lives; more audibly, it seemed, for us than for them.

Nineteen

All losses are difficult and the loss of a baby or child seems particularly cruel because it is too early. The nature of SIDS means that it has its own specific layers of distress. There is no answer to the question "what caused my baby to die?"

There is a second question that hovers and haunts when any child dies. Why *my* child?

In 1990 Christopher Davis and Camille Wortman and their colleagues interviewed 124 parents whose babies had died of SIDS.[6] They talked to them three times – two-to-four weeks, three months, and eighteen months, after their babies had died. Most of these bereaved parents looked for some way to make sense of the death of their baby.

---

[6] Davis & Wortman 2000 Searching for Meaning in Loss: Are clinical assumptions correct? *Death Studies* 24, 497-540.

The benefits of holding a religious belief were found to be strong. Those who described themselves as religious were not just more likely to find some meaning in their loss; they also scored highly on measures of wellbeing. If you believe, for example, that God wanted your baby for Himself or that your child's death happened in order that another soul might come into the world there is, it appears, some comfort. These accounts do not explain what caused a child to die, but they do offer some reasons why it might have happened. They may help to answer the 'Why *my* child?' question.

Some parents embrace a kind of spiritualism that is not Christian. In a recent book called *How Can I Keep Breathing?*[7] the author, Olivia Sunshine, says that the book is co-authored by her son Ben, one of her 'angels', twenty-six years after he died at the age of five. Part Two of the book is a conversation between Olivia and Ben in 2011, facilitated by clairvoyance. This book calls for a vigorous belief in the power of mediums, a belief I do not share. Sunshine has a robust and enduring belief in life after death, although she does not invoke God as part of that belief system.

I hold a strong respect for the right of people to hold these beliefs, especially as they are often (although not always) comforting. But I had rejected the comforts of religious belief and of life after death in some form. No-one could tell me what had caused Alexander to die, nor why he in particular had died. I created my own framework for explaining the cause of his death, relying on a different kind of faith – that science would

---

[7] *How Can I Keep Breathing?* Olivia Sunshine. Balboa Press, 2013.

someday unravel the cause. I know now that the framework I built was approximately the same as the scientific understanding is at the time of my writing. In an approximate but good-enough way, I made sense of the loss at the time. And because I believed in science, and did not imagine a god making decisions about individual babies, I did not feel the need to ask 'Why *my* child?'

* * *

A crucial aspect of becoming a grown-up is developing a set of beliefs about the world and how it works. We need to do that or we would constantly be wondering why the world is the way it is, or even whether it is as it seems. Those enquiries can be exhausting and can absorb more time than most people have to spare so mostly we come to some working conclusions. If something happens that makes us question whether or not they are right, we have to revise those conclusions. We then go about adapting, bringing them into our world-view and adjusting it accordingly.

So we come to a working understanding of how things are. We know the sun rises and sets. We believe that almost always other drivers will stay on their side of the road. We take for granted, at least in western countries, that the price we see on cauliflowers and dresses is what we will have to pay. We assume that our partners will for the most part behave in the ways we have come to know and understand. We believe that the people who love us have our best interests at heart.

And we assume that our babies will not die.

When a baby dies without warning the assumptions and beliefs parents have are thrown up and out. Babies *do* die, the world is not as benevolent and safe as we thought. Somehow we have to re-order our framework of understanding of the world. It takes a long time, and it is not easy.

Reframing my world happened in a haphazard way that makes sense only as I look back on it. First, I noticed that what used to matter no longer mattered so much. Several weeks after Alexander's death, we were driving in Germany on the *autobahn* in our ageing Volkswagen camper van. Darkness was falling and we lumbered along, being passed by tiny Fiats as we peered at exit signs written in a language neither Jim nor I could read. Simon and Emily were tired. 'Are we nearly there?' I was navigating as ineptly as I usually did, panicking at my inability to get us off this race track. If it had happened months before, my conversation with Jim would have been through two sets of gritted teeth. Not this time. I realised that it just didn't matter. Well, it did matter, we were lost in the dark in a strange country. But we were not going to die, we would find a way. The fact that we were lost and had no immediate way of finding ourselves fell down the ranking of what was important in the wider context of our lives, which meant I could calm down – a little – and focus on navigating rather than over-reacting.

If the house was a mess, I relaxed into it rather than going into a frenzy of unfocused tidying. If the rice went claggy when friends were with us for dinner, I didn't care. Neither did they.

After Alexander

I was getting what matters into perspective.

What mattered, fiercely; what clambered to the top of the hierarchy of mattering, was the wellbeing of Simon and Emily. Their preciousness and their vulnerability shouted at me daily, at full volume. I no longer took their existence for granted. It would not be true to say that I became a gentle, all-forgiving mother, and nor was I hyper-vigilant. I just *noticed* them more, told them more often how much I loved them. I appreciated them more.

Something else happened. I have always been enraptured by birds. Tough, fragile, lightweight frames moving with panache through space, exquisite judgment as they swirl with each other, land perfectly on branches, sing their hopes and dreams to the world. Now I started to be increasingly entranced by other ciphers of perfection – a line of trees, the curve of a child's cheek, the grace of a running cat, the sweetness of a snatch of music. These day-to-day minutiae, these familiar miracles, became extraordinary. Trivia became at the same time both exquisite and deeply unimportant.

These things of the world were highlighted and inestimably beautiful in those weeks and months as I grieved Alexander.

* * *

A more discomforting realisation began to emerge. My identity, my sense of self, was being challenged by what had happened.

I had thought that I was a capable parent with the ability to keep my children safe, that I was at least a good-enough mother. Alexander's death confronted these assumptions. The process of demolishing and then rebuilding a sense of confidence, a self that I can live comfortably with, started then, and is still a work in progress. It has been a fundamental reconstruction, using some of the wholesome blocks that remained, and discarding many more that were not.

Five years after Alexander's death an image formed in my mind, appearing at moments when my brain was idling in neutral. It was not a dream, and neither was it a vision in any usual sense of that term. I was looking at a woman at the bottom of a dry well, sitting on a concrete pad that prevented her from falling any lower. I realised she was me. I was naked, my head was on my knees, and it was clear that there was nothing left of me to judge. Old layers had been stripped away like the silvery parts of an onion, leaving an indestructible kernel. The only way to manoeuvre was upwards, the only way to rebuild was to replace stripped layers with great care, to re-clothe myself with new, carefully examined garb. There was no hurry. The great beauty, the revelation in all this, was that the naked, fundamental woman was not open to evaluation. She was just what she was, and she had the option to clothe herself with new attire that fitted the self that she was becoming.

So a subterranean reorganisation had begun. In the past a persistent, insistent, tape had played in my head – so familiar that I had ceased to attend to it. I started to listen in.

"You're a bit overweight." My BMI hovered just above skinny.

"You're not as clever as you think." I had scored A passes in all my postgraduate papers.

"You're a neglectful mother, studying when you should be looking after your children." My children were apparently happy and well-adjusted, and still are.

"You are a hopeless housewife." That one was true.

I turned the tape off, smashed the recorder, and enjoyed the silence.

* * *

'How do you feel?' This question came from a counsellor, as our marriage began to fray.

'I don't know.' This was more serious. Decades of trying to behave acceptably had wedged a soundproof slab between things that happened to me and my emotional responses. It would be twenty-four hours after someone said something troubling or annoying that I would register irritation. Levering out that wedge took even more effort than smashing the recorder. I have to remain vigilant – that slab falls all too easily back into place.

All this happened, over a long time and slowly. The change was almost indiscernible in a short timeframe; over months and years it has become visible and real. I am on quiet alert. It is forever vulnerable, this self that has emerged.

As I write this, I wonder what others around me noticed. Was this excruciatingly slow reconstruction obvious? For me - the person being rebuilt - the process barely reached consciousness. I was aware of confusion and dislocation, buried under the day-to-day weight of a life that demanded that my roles as a mother, partner, and scholar function even as they were undergoing renovation.

No doubt it was difficult for those I loved and who loved me. The *fact* that I changed was less painful than the impact the underground changes were having on my behaviour. I suspect I was at times belligerent, confused, contradictory and distracted – unfortunate precursors to pulling myself together. I was also becoming more gentle, more peaceful and coherent as the process continued.

The rebuild is far from perfect. Over two decades later the voice of the tape still begins to murmur if I am not vigilant. The difference is that now I hear it, and I know how to push the off button.

Two decades later, a sliver of the wedge still slips between my feelings and the events that provoke them. It is more readily dislodged because I know it is there.

That is the difference. I can re-call the woman in the well, remind myself that her layers are not made of the same stuff as her core. That core has aspects that are not all attractive, but they are mine and I accept them. I can be more myself. Being more myself means I feel more resilient, I am more independent, I am stronger. I am not better than I was, nor am I worse. But I know a lot more about who I am and why. I am both less self-critical and more tolerant of others. That is a gift, albeit an imperfect improvement.

Twenty

In 1981 I knew nothing about any processes of grief. Working through Alexander's loss followed no formula. Our hearts and minds flowed in the chaotic border-crossing way that happens in real life, circling and back-tracking, slowing and accelerating. Now I am able to step back from the raw, unprocessed and unsupported experience we went through and to take a look at what others have said about mourning.

It's a universal and usually messy business, this grieving. Many great and not-so-great minds have tested themselves by trying to explain what it is and how we should go about doing it. Here are a few of the main ideas.

First, Freud. He wrote a paper in 1917 called *Mourning and Melancholia*[8]. It is almost the only musing he did on mourning, and in it he compared it with melancholia, or depression. He

---

[8] S. Freud: *Mourning and Melancholia*. Zeitschrift, vol.4, 1917.

listed the similarities – many – and a key difference. Mourning does not include a significant and persistent plummet in self-regard, as melancholia does. His terminology is unique; he says that in the process of mourning, a person withdraws 'libido' (Freud used this term to encompass every instinct which may be described as love) or psychic energy from the love object (i.e. the dead person), by summoning each and every memory of the person and hypercathecting it. Hypercathexis means an over-involvement or overinvestment of libido in something or someone.

In more simple language, Freud is saying that in order to grieve a lost loved one, effectively we must put all our emotional energy into remembering everything about that person, and then we must let those memories go.

Freud's suggestion is that only after the over-involvement in the memories of the person can we return to reality. This is not easy – it involves grief work in which the mourner revisits every memory and thought of the loved person and detaches from them. When mourning is complete, the ego becomes free and uninhibited again. Only then is energy retrieved to invest in other relationships. Over-investment in mourning passes over time; with melancholia it persists. *Not* to do this work is to fail to grieve normally.

Soon before Emily was born, I wondered if I would have sufficient love (or libido in Freud's terminology) left over from the mountains of it heaped on Simon, to give to her. I was imagining that love is somehow a finite quantity. The moment she was born, however, I fell in love with her, without withdrawing any of the love I had for Simon. I discovered that love is an infinite resource. The implication, then, that I would need to retrieve what I had poured into Alexander in order to have a supply for other relationships does not fit with my experience. With the exception of the apparently finite nature of libido, however, the visiting of connections with Alexander - and if not letting them go, then transforming them into something that fitted with the reality that he had died – makes some sense.

Throughout his paper, Freud is at pains to point out that evidence for his theory is sparse and that he is simply observing what happens. It is not, then, prescriptive. Freud is not telling us *how* to mourn.

A very famous attempt to impose structure on the chaos that is mourning, and to impose a structure on it, emerged in the mid-twentieth century. This is the work of Elisabeth Kübler-Ross.[9]

Imagine, if you can, being one of a set of triplets. Three girls: Elisabeth, Erika, and Eva. They were born in Switzerland into a culture devoted to the work ethic. Imagine, too, being a clever woman in this environment and time when "man" meant both women and men but in professional contexts mostly men. She was nurtured in a family medium that fostered a sense of commitment and competitiveness, and as a woman and a triplet she had the extra determination to be heard and understood.

---

[9] I am indebted to the book *The Truth About Grief* by Ruth Davis Konisberg (Simon & Schuster, 2011), for raising my awareness of the life of EKR.

She studied medicine in Zurich, met and married an American fellow student, and moved to the United States. There, after holding several positions in hospitals, she began interviewing dying patients first in Denver, and then in Chicago. She used open-ended questions to elicit responses, asked different questions of each patient, and interviewed each person just once. She had an audience of medical students and colleagues. Her aim – she succeeded in this – was to raise the awareness of health professionals to the fact that the sick and dying bodies in their care were also human beings with feelings and fears, confronting their mortality.

Her sessions became both popular and famous. An editorial assistant at publishers MacMillan read an article Kübler-Ross had written about her work, and invited her to write a book about dying. There is a special excitement in being asked to write a first book, and she agreed. She was, though, given a very tight time-frame and she found herself brainstorming alone at night, trying to impose some structure to her material. This musing under pressure led her to perceive patterns in the interviews she had carried out, and to describe the stages for which she is now so famous. There is some suggestion that her framework was not entirely original; others, it seems, had described similar processes before she did. They, though, did not publish or become well-known outside medical circles.

According to the Kübler-Ross model, we follow the DABDA sequence for grieving: denial, anger, bargaining, depression and acceptance. These steps are assumed to be sequential, and one stage has to be experienced and resolved before moving on to the next. Her model offered structure and a pre-determined path to follow. Failure to do so was to fail at grieving. It provided a framework within which grief counsellors and others working with death and dying could guide the grieving process.

It is problematic. First, it was based on interviews not with grieving people but with those who themselves were dying. Yet today its application is overwhelmingly to those who have lost someone beloved. And the "evidence" for it is weak – just one conversation with each person; no validation or verification or any of the other testing of theories that give us some confidence that they are at least partly true. And in contrast to Freud, she took the leap from describing what she had seen and heard, to prescribing what *should* happen.

The simplicity of her framework was both breathtaking and attractive. It was seized upon and promoted by grief counsellors; one size, it was assumed, would fit all sorrow. The simplification of something that is complex and messy, as grieving is, has strong but misleading appeal.

In the days and weeks after Alexander's death, I was angry. I lashed out at the hapless woman in Boots. I entertained blame – mostly of myself but also of others like the unfortunate anaesthetist in the ambulance. And I came to an acceptance of losing Alexander. I did not deny that he had died, although I wished fervently I could stop time and reverse it. Nor did I become depressed. Three out of five – ABA. Blame was holding hands with anger, it was not following it in a line. My responses were a stew rather than a neat, linear progression.

Almost all grand theories have some partial truths in them and Kübler-Ross's model has had a wide following, perhaps because it was the first to impose some structure on the common chaos of grief.

I found another intriguing framework, made easy to remember by the mnemonic RRRRRR – the Six R model. The author is also an R – Rando.[10] Like that of Elisabeth Kübler-Ross, his model has phases:

Recognise
React
Recollect
Relinquish
Readjust
Reinvent

Had I known about Rando, I would have struggled. I would not have been able to remember all six Rs at the time of Alexander's death, nor the order in which I was supposed to address them. I am glad I did not know.

Both Kübler-Ross and Rando make similar assumptions. First, that successful grieving calls for work – hard, focused work. Second, that there is a right way to do it – follow the DABDA

---

[10] Terese Rando. *How to Go on Living When Someone You Love Dies.* Lexington Books, 1991.

routine, tick off the six Rs. Still today, the majority of grief counsellors work with one or another model that is prescriptive.

Like many theoretical frameworks, those of Kübler-Ross and Rando hold some gems of insight. The problem with them is in the application – they are grasped by counsellors and individuals and treated as the Truth about how to mourn. The process of mourning is as diverse as the people who go through it.

In the late 1990s, a freshly minted Ph.D graduate from Yale named George Bonanno[11] wrought considerable damage to these frameworks when he discovered, to his own astonishment and the scepticism of others, that nearly half of a non-clinical sample of grieving spouses showed what he termed resilience. These widows and widowers were not pathological; they were not denying their loss or their grief. They were not following prescribed patterns of mourning. What they were showing was the ability, to quote Bonanno: "to maintain relatively stable, healthy levels of psychological and physical functioning", as well as "the capacity for generative experiences and positive emotions" in the face of loss and sadness.

Unlike previous claims, Bonanno's findings were supported by sound research – dispassionate, replicable, and reliable. He did not provide a model for how we should properly grieve,

---

[11] Bonanno: 'Loss, Trauma, and Human Resilience: Have we underestimated the Human Capacity to Thrive After Extremely Aversive Events?' *American Psychologist 59, no.1* (January 2004). 20-28.

although he did describe four trajectories of grief that he noted in his research. The first is *resilience*, found in the majority of his sample.

The second trajectory is *recovery*, when normal functioning temporarily gives way to significant distress, usually for a period of at least several months, and then gradually returns to the level of functioning that the person had before their loss.

The third is *chronic dysfunction*, when there is prolonged suffering and inability to function, usually lasting several years or longer.

The fourth is *delayed grief or trauma*, when adjustment seems normal but then distress and symptoms increase months later.

My adult life has been focused on research. I put my faith in explanations that are based on evidence rather than speculation. Just as persuasively, Bonanno's description of resilient grieving fits my experience exactly. I sustained, I had to sustain, relatively stable levels of functioning. I had two children who needed me to be that way. And positive emotions such as joy emerged surprisingly soon after Alexander's death.

Bonanno's observation that the straitjacket of stage models such as that of Kübler-Ross is not the experience of most bereaved people freed theorists to consider models that encompass individual responses and messy pathways. One of these is the Dual Process Model[12], which suggests that when bereaved, people oscillate between a state of loss and grieving, and one of coping and restoration of day-to-day life.

As I came to the end of writing this chapter, I found a paper describing a framework called 'Grief to Personal Growth'. It was written in 2002. Here is a quote from the first section:

"Personal growth is an outcome of the grieving process, a time when the bereaved are having more good than bad days. They have recreated a new sense of self that is more compassionate toward others and more forgiving and more tolerant of themselves and others. They have overcome the hopelessness that defined earlier grief and now have a fundamentally optimistic outlook for their future. These reconstructions of meaning reveal their changed self-identity and worldview."[13]

The authors might have been looking over my shoulder as they built this framework and tested it. I did not need to understand the structural equation modelling they used to develop their model, to recognise the rightness in what they were saying. They were writing about *my* emergence and transformation.

---

[12] Dual Process Model: Stroebe, M, & Schut, H. The dual process model of coping with bereavement: rationale and description. *Death Studies* 1999; 23 (3) 197-224.

[13] Hogan, N.S. & Schmidt, L. A. (2002). Testing the Grief to Personal Growth Model Using Structural Equation Modeling. *Death Studies* 26: 615-634.

It encapsulates my experience, sums up in seventy-four words what it took me over three decades to recognise and name.

My experience has been that there is more to grieving than simply returning to "normal". That realisation has been a strong motive for writing this book. And in grief literature there is an emerging view that the process can be and often is transformative, as bringing about changes in a bereaved person that are fundamental and life-changing, and often positive.

I have written this memoir as a mother who lost a son, and as a scholar whose professional life has focused on understanding the relationships amongst children and those who love them. As I have written, links and themes have revealed themselves that would have stayed hidden had I either retained the perspective of a scholar, or confined myself to the lens of a bereaved parent.

The writing about Alexander and his impact on the family and my life has brought into the light a process that was happening underground. Its uncovering has brought together what I had perceived only diffusely – the movement from shock to despair to hope to redemption to self-acceptance – with what actually happened. The writing has revealed the invisible ink of those years of processing.

Man (and presumably woman), said Victor Frankl, has a fundamental drive to find meaning in life. It is a primary motivation, a *will* to meaning.[14] For Frankl, his will to hold fast to meaning in his life enabled him to survive Nazi concentration camps where others who saw no hope in their lives lit cigarettes, lay down on their beds, and died. Frankl speaks of a sense of "tragic optimism", a stance he describes as "saying yes to life in spite of everything".

The death of a baby or the survival of the Holocaust are not required as a prerequisite for embarking on a quest for what life – one's life – means. Millions of people question the significance of their lives when those lives have never experienced disaster.

Neither does major loss or trauma necessarily precipitate an inquisition into what it all means. For many, meaning is already defined in their lives through religious or spiritual belief. And for some people, the questions simply do not arise.

I do not remember asking myself what my life meant or how it had changed after Alexander died. It is as I look back, remember, reflect, and join some dots, that I recognise the progressions his death set in train.

I was not diminished. I was not destroyed. I have emerged a different person from the one I would have been had he not died. Surviving and ultimately thriving after a shocking loss has involved making sense of Alexander's death, of

---

[14] Victor Frankl: *Man's Search for Meaning*. P. 137

reconfiguring my world- and self-views, and of discovering reservoirs of resilience and strength that were unsuspected. I am not just back to normal, I am more than I was before he died.

The term "vulnerable optimism" works for me. It describes the blending of sorrow and grief, the discovery of strength, the feeling of authenticity, and the forgiveness of myself and others and the space I find myself occupying now. It describes the paradox of mixing hopefulness with the ever-present awareness that present blessings may disappear.

I am vulnerable. I know that babies die. I am on high alert, around other people's babies, with my grandchildren. I hide that hyper-alertness; it is mine, not theirs. Simultaneously, to survive Alexander's death and to thrive is to know that one can endure lesser tragedies.

I am optimistic. My world is rich with life, both new and mature. The acute awareness of a bean seed sprouting, a blackbird singing, my cat settling precisely on my lap, a perfect string quartet movement, is a form of appreciation I have learned through coming to comprehend that perfection is both exquisite and terribly fragile.

Strength and vulnerability come together yin and yang-like in what feels like a coherent whole to face the positives and the negatives of my life. They do not make me a "happier" person. They make me a more authentic one.

Self-knowledge is precious. I know how fainthearted I am; I went limp when Alexander was unconscious. I know how uncharitable I can be; I blamed the ambulance driver for not going faster. I know that I am both deeply fallible and remarkably robust. This is a story of resilience that followed from grief and survival, and from the emergence of joy and gratitude for Alexander's 107 days.

I have learned from Alexander to say yes to life.

(I have) an awareness of the profound sadness flowing from Alex's death that shaped a lot of our family history, but that also made us very tight knit in a lot of ways. I appreciate what an amazing family I do have more and more.

Letter from Simon, 2014

Twenty-One

The memory of him is not so much an image of his physical body – after all, at six months he would be a very different baby – but of the feelings of warmth and joy associated with his laughs and smiles. They are the moments remembered by us all, which involved him and were enriched by him. His memory, too, is in the tenderness and awareness of babies showing so strongly in Simon and Emily. Diary, July 1981

The Cambridge seminars had receded into the category of too-hard-to-contemplate in the weeks after Alexander died. Gradually, though, I began to crave diversion from the enervating moping that occupied the days in the house alone. I decided to go up to Cambridge again. On a Tuesday morning in June I started the Volkswagen van and drove out through the lanes that led through the villages of southern Cambridgeshire to the outskirts of Cambridge. In 1981, parking was easy to find on the streets around the city centre.

I walked to Free School Lane light, floating with the unburden of my baby. I felt undressed.

I sat in the room with the wide, high windows, wondering how sensible it was to be there. Would I be able to endure a whole hour of someone talking dispassionately about children's development? Or would I become an unseemly shambles if anyone offered sympathy?

Janet, the elderly paediatrician, took me into an office. Her voice had the calmness of someone skilled at gentling fretful babies. She talked to me about the current theories about why babies die of cot death. Allergy to cow's milk was one, and Alexander had been given yoghurt for the first time in the hour before he became unconscious. My ever-ready guilt-prone self leapt to attention. Had we caused his death when we spooned that creamy lactose-ridden delight into his mouth? That theory, I have discovered, has not been supported by evidence.

After the seminar, Martin Richards came over to me, his limp slowing his progress across the room.

'If I'd had a baby who died of cot death, I would want to know why it had happened,' he said. 'I know some of the people who are doing research in England into its causes. I can introduce you if you like. And my library has all the publications from the last five years. Go through them if it would help.'

His offer was perfect. He was giving me, a doubter of common beliefs, a chance to examine the ostensibly impartial faith of science.

His library was a windowless room shelved with monographs, papers, numbered boxes and books about research in child development. On a desk was an unruly folder with an index that told me which boxes contained which papers. The system was like Martin – mildly messy but underpinned with a logic that was impressive.

I did not contact the researchers. I combed the scientific papers, written in the spare prose of academia. No mellifluous phrases, no hints of emotion. Each paper had a comforting structure - abstract, introduction, method, results, conclusions. Their conclusions have essentially not changed over time. No-one knows what causes babies to stop breathing in their sleep and to die.

The science could not answer my need for an explanation of Alexander's death. Neither did it pretend. It spoke of puzzlement and of a commitment to understanding this most mysterious of fatal conditions.

* * *

We were in Cornwall with Barbara and Iain, on a holiday long ago planned to include two new babies as well as the older cousins, Simon and Emily and Anna. The house we had rented, Medla, sat assertively on the cliff in New Polzeath, as it has done now for over a hundred years. Its rooms encompassed light and space, with huge bay windows overlooking the summer sea. Along the cliffs, wildflowers flourished in the sun. The air smelled of salt and midsummer. Our two young families and Jim's parents spread into the contours of the house flowing into the living area and out into the private spaces.

I sat in an armchair with my back to the bay window, holding three-month-old Jonathan. I clutched, rocked, and gazed into his face. I felt his weight, a baby-sized heft in my arms. I ached for Alexander, rubbed my eyes with my fists, and held Jonathan harder. Emily and Simon played board games with their grandparents, glancing at their mother who was nursing their small cousin, passing him to their father, and taking him back again.

For Barbara and Iain, that time must have been like stepping through scorpions. How could they know what to do for us? Should they hide Jonathan away? Should they apologise, somehow, for his birth? With exquisite selflessness they set aside their need to celebrate their baby boy for the time we were there. He was ours to hold and love. With consummate sensitivity, with grace and love, they navigated our unpredictable responses.

The experience of being with Jonathan for two weeks in Cornwall was salutary. He was a baby – warm and wriggling and just right to have on a knee and in arms. He was not Alexander and he felt and acted differently. So the distinction was clearly there between a baby and Alexander. He also cried, filled his nappies, and offered a worthwhile reminder that babies can be inconvenient.

I did not know then how important this distinction, unarticulated and deep, was soon to become. That Jonathan was not Alexander, that babies are distinctively themselves, was to be the underpinning of the ability to move out from under an undiscriminating place of loss and longing.

* * *

... more and more often it is possible to appreciate and hold to oneself the precious fact that Alexander ever existed – even if that existence led to the body blow of losing him. The awareness of the rose-tinted-glasses phenomenon does not stop me from remembering him as loving and laughing and lively, twinkling and grinning and extracting every ounce of experience from his brief existence. And wondrous – his total marvellous little body was summed up for me by the magic of his ear and all its intricacy. What was the miracle that enabled us to create such a perfect little body? He did cry, and have dirty nappies, and want to be carried when I needed two hands, and wake me at night. But he reached out with his hands and feet and smiles to experience every moment of living that he could. Diary, June 1981

Another change was stirring beneath the mess of my sad self. I began to feel lucky. The focus on the raw pain of loss was softening. I was able to think of Alexander and to smile at the memory of his sense of fun. Simon and Emily and I talked about his baby chuckle when they had bounced him on the bed. We sang his song together, the one we sang to him in Paris – 'Eeh er man he has two feet to walk down the stre-e-et!'

Tentacles of light, shy slivers of respite from gloom, were seeping through. They broached my darkness with tenderness.

I began to be glad for his short existence, to feel lucky I had had my baby.

Joy was creeping in to join sorrow in the remembering. It set off an oscillation between the two poles of sadness and happiness. The swinging subsided as I began to understand that having had Alexander in our lives was a blessing. So began a gentle progression from despair to gratitude.

I have a friend with whom I shared some of my most undressed, raw feelings in the weeks after Alexander died. I have never met her. Her name is Carol. She lives in Scotland, and we have a mutually beloved friend who joined our letter-writing hands. Our experiences and responses were of similar shapes and hues. Carol's daughter had died of SIDS seven years earlier than Alexander and she reprised her own responses at the same time as she wrote to console me. She said:

... recently I was with a nine-week-old baby and naturally she reminded me of Alice, and inevitably I felt how great had been our loss when she died – and the feeling came over me that such a sentiment no longer was relevant, and how fortunate we had been to have had her at all. The switch of emotion wasn't a result of the very necessary positive thinking of earlier days, but one that overcame me with a sense of wellbeing. I count myself very fortunate indeed.

Waking up in the morning started to feel different. My legs were not so weighted, my eyes let the daylight in with less protest. The anticipation of coffee resumed its sweet imperative.

Part of me was dismayed. I did not want to get over Alexander. It worried me. If I was to "get over it", if I stopped feeling devastated, if I "let him go", even if I simply began to adapt, would I start to forget him? That would be a betrayal. Part of me wanted to pull my despair more closely around my shoulders, to prevent memories from leaking out, to stop them from bleaching in the light the chinks let in.

It felt a weighty responsibility, this not-forgetting, this holding memories fresh and close. No-one knew him quite as well as I had done, and I had to hold him from sliding away into oblivion. No-one in New Zealand had met him so our memories were the only evidence of his living that would affirm his existence. They were his life after death. Others at home could only imagine him, look at the fuzzy photographs of a small baby who might have been any baby. There would be no grave, no casket of ashes, nothing tangible. The brief life of Alexander would leave its mark only in the hearts of those who loved him. We owed him at least that – to keep his memories intact.

Carol wrote:
(Re-reading what I have written) I see I have equated 'forget' with being less distressed by the fact of the death. If I had realised that seven years ago, it would have helped.

This was what was happening for me. As distress began to lose its pungency, I mistook its recession for beginning to forget Alexander. The ebbing grief was in fact clearing some space for gratitude and a more clear-sighted appreciation of his life.

Twenty-Two

For the first week after Alexander died my body longed for a baby – a physiological yearning which has abated considerably, leaving the emotional/psychological factors to be sorted out. At first the longing for Alex, the need for a baby, etc, all jumbled in together; gradually the time to mourn for Alex for himself is separating him out from the general desire to have a baby around. The person, Alexander, is increasingly distinct from baby in general, and I <u>think</u> it would be legitimate to replace baby in general so long as that is not a disguise for replacing Alex in particular.   Diary, July 1981

The invasion of light stepped up. The hollows in my heart began to morph from desolate holes to light spaces that were aching for a baby in my arms again. They were aching not for the baby that was Alexander, but for *a* baby. Yet to contemplate the possibility of another child was to look in the other direction, down a path strewn with barbed wire. Three months after Alexander's death, I peered at the entrance of this pathway.

It was happening for Jim, too. At breakfast one morning he asked:

'How do you feel about having another baby?'

A jumble of responses assembled themselves, incoherent. *I don't want to forget Alexander. I don't want to replace Alexander. Maybe it's too early?*

'I don't know,' I said.

And I didn't know. We had not talked to each other much about how we felt about all that had happened; I was less ready than Jim was to make the freighted decision to have another baby. One part of me felt compelled toward what felt like an inevitability. The other dragged itself unwillingly toward the possibility of heartbreak that would have, I thought, killed me.

It was a slow progression along stepping-stones that moved me toward distinguishing Alexander from all babies, and any future baby from Alexander. They were steps that were taking me to the capacity to see another child as a person in its own right. At the time they were a jumble of paving blocks, circling around and back on themselves, leading nowhere in particular. What I knew was that the feelings and thoughts needed to be disentangled so that I felt safe enough to step out and away from the circling. And that called for time, and for information.

* * *

I had been certain I had had enough babies. And because I knew that babies did not die, I was happily intending to end all chance of having more. Had Alexander died a few days later I would have been intentionally and irretrievably infertile, tubes safely knotted. That wonder of timing meant that I could still conceive although my age meant that the chances were diminishing. I was thirty-four.

The fact of the timing of Alexander's death could have been another siren call to believe in the intervention of fate, to believe in God or his representatives. It could easily have been a reinforcement of the "it was meant to be" mantra.

How tempting it might have been to believe that Someone, Something, was meddling in my life by timing his death so close to the knots in my tubes being tied. And to pursue that line of reasoning, any new baby would have been "meant to be". It would be a cruel responsibility to load onto a child, a burden to somehow perform because of his or her predestination.

I was not tempted to think like this. Nonetheless, the fact of being able to have another baby would shimmer forever as an enigma. He or she was astonishingly close to not being able to be conceived.

So we *could* have another baby. But could we survive another cot death? I was certain we could not.

We visited Dr Dimwiddie, a neonatal paediatrician.

'Yes, there is a slightly increased risk of a cot death if you've already had one.'

'How much risk?' Jim asked.

'One to two per cent.'

I have never known how to respond to risk statistics. It depends on why you want to know. If I am buying a lotto ticket, a one-in-one-hundred chance of winning makes it worth the punt – there's only the ticket price to lose. If I am considering, as we were, the chances of having another baby die, it gives pause. So I called the Cot Death Society in London.

The woman on the phone had a voice laced with quiet authority.

'Have you had any other children, Jan?'

'Yes, we have Simon and Emily, they are seven and five.'

'Then your risk of having another baby die of cot death is really insignificant. Your other two are fine. I wouldn't worry.'

My rational self cheered.

My stomach quaked at the prospect of any risk at all.

* * *

... it is terribly frightening to contemplate the strength I know will be needed to get through the fears – the fear of abnormality, fear of labour problems, and of course another infant death. The knowledge of their irrationality does not make them very much less. More time is needed to strengthen both the conviction that I won't be attempting to replace Alex, and the resolve to get through the fears. Diary, July 1981

Jim and I decided to find out more, this time from an obstetrician.

Colin Sims had a voice that was soft and reassuring. We discussed the physical and, to a lesser extent, the emotional aspects of another child. He questioned us about the possibility of looking for a replacement baby. Our responses convinced him and he removed the loop that was preventing us from conceiving. My immediate feeling was one of flatness. It was certainly not wild elation, but it felt like another small step toward healing. It was a glimmer of the possibility of a great happiness, a possibility that I knew must be approached with infinite care and caution.

Uppermost was the sense that it removed Alexander, my beautiful son, a little further into history. I was fairly confident, though, that another child would never change or diminish his place in our lives, and that maybe its life would be enhanced a little by what Alexander had given us.

* * *

It happened fast. As soon as the loop stopped obstructing the linking of the parts needed for making a baby, I was pregnant. The chances of conceiving in the first month or two of trying are modest for anyone. For us they were vanishingly small. One of my fallopian tubes had been blasted into nonexistence by an ectopic pregnancy in 1973 that had - statistically - reduced the likelihood of conception by fifty per cent. I had envisaged months of unstressed time trying to conceive, months in which to assimilate our decision to have another child and to let it take form and shape in our lives.

But I was pregnant again with only two or three weeks to anticipate its impact. Inside me, minuscule, was another life. It embodied the same vulnerability that goes with all newly-conceived embryos – risk of miscarriage, genes gone awry and attaching wrong bits to DNA strands, two faces on one body, brain forming outside the cranium. I knew about these possibilities – they were remote, and they were not my worry. Mine was far more intangible, saturating me inside and out. What if this baby was normal, lived to be born and loved, and then died on my watch as Alexander had done? The fear did not fit into the box of disembodied anxiety; it had happened, it was real, it was impossible to consign to the regions of remote improbability. And there was no test for cot death. It would not show up on scans, it was not detectable by genetic tests.

Becoming pregnant so quickly felt like getting on an international flight soon after a major plane disaster. The odds were good, but crashes happen. A journey had begun a little too soon, one that was unstoppable and soaked with possibilities for both grief and joy.

* * *

Our time in Bygrave was dwindling. The village started a round of farewell dinners that fattened our bodies and softened our leaving. Simon and Emily were not pleased. They had adapted to life in England, in the village, and half-forgotten New Zealand. They resented having to leave.

'How,' Simon asked, 'can you take me away from the country where I was born?'

Jim and I went to Paris alone for a last continental weekend, leaving Simon and Emily with Vellyn and David. We woke in our three-star hotel not on children time but when our bodies were ready. We submerged ourselves in galleries and cafés, listened to free organ recitals, and wandered the now familiar alleys of the city. It was early August, and we promenaded in the dusky evenings with locals and tourists across Pont Neuf, along Boulevard St-Michel. The bombshell in my tummy permeated our talk and our thoughts, the new life we had created that held such weight for our future. My awareness of the baby was heightened by the marinade of nausea in which I was soaking. The odours of the markets we loved were repugnant, the effort to appreciate the glory of Notre-Dame was diluted through the lens of morning sickness. Jim experienced all Paris offered with clarity and delight. I hugged my belly.

As we landed back in London, smog came down, dulling the silver air to grey. We could smell, feel, taste it. I found myself trying to decide which was worse - to stop breathing until we drove out of this poisoned air and so deprive the baby of oxygen, or to inhale toxic particles and risk contaminating it. My body gave me no choice. It needed oxygen. So I breathed, holding one of Jim's partly-used handkerchiefs over my mouth.

* * *

High summer in Bygrave. Skylarks were lacing the sky, and on the ground they lured two- and four-legged threats away from their nests by feigning broken wings. School had finished, so children's chatter ebbed and flowed up and down the lane in the afternoons and the long, light evenings. And it was time for us to leave. We combined last and second-last visits to London with dispatching boxes back to New Zealand. Muffin's spaniel brain told her that something was changing. She glued herself to the nearest set of heels that passed her nose, flitting frantically from person to person. Simon and Emily pretended it was not happening.

'Can I go and play with Ben, Mum?'

'Of course, love. Enjoy yourself – we are leaving next week.'

'Don't say that!'

The day came. Dave, a neighbour, drove his Audi into the curving driveway. Suitcases were stuffed into the boot. Simon and Emily ran down the lane in a frenzy of goodbyes to their friends. Two sulky child bodies were loaded into the back seat, their mother wedged in between. Resentment swirled through the rear of the car. Jim sat in the front seat with Dave as we moved slowly down the lane, waving at neighbours we would never see again. It was a strange echo of our arrival ten months earlier – four New Zealanders with baby-on-board, the two events separated by a year of friendship and fun and tragedy and love.

Twenty-Three

Our first stop on the way back to New Zealand was Crete. In the early 1980s it was a dusty island with modest roads that were littered with rental villas and unassertive high-rise buildings. There were villages where the inhabitants still wept and hugged us when they found we were from New Zealand. World War Two was recent, for them. We had scoured the travel brochures that everyone in England devours after Christmas when images of beaches and sunlight offer distant hope of escape from the darkest days of the year. We had booked a flat in the Cristi apartment block on the northern coast near Hersonissou, thirty miles east of Heraklion.

The block was a bunker, set in a coastal landscape scattered with the concrete bones of imminent hotels stalled in their growth. It no longer exists; it is replaced with glistening high-rise apartments that encourage the gaze over the sea rather than as it was then, looking across arid red tracks leading into the scruffy hillocks behind the road. It felt like the dawning of a tourist explosion and it was, but we were there in the happy, ramshackle days when the locals were willing to engage with us. Our fellow tourists on similar packages of flights and accommodation were mostly from northern England. Smoke issued continuously from their noses; after a day in the sun they sported red necks that, we discovered when we talked to them, matched their political views. In front of the block the sea was sensationally blue, tawny sand joining with the ripples fluttering at its edge.

My mother joined us. She had been on a European sojourn, travelling in air-conditioned buses on tours where she wore a label saying "Hello, my name is Sylvia".

She had made her own arrangements to fly to Heraklion Airport. We had sent instructions to get her from there to our apartment, and suggested she get a taxi. Her plane was due to land at 9.00pm but by midnight she had not arrived at Cristi, so we called the airport. Someone answered, perhaps a cleaner, who was there after the last flight had landed and the airport had closed. Remarkably, the voice on the phone understood my accented English. No, madam, there is no-one here that looks like an elderly woman with too much luggage. We went to bed, envisioning my unfortunate mother lying on the ground somewhere, relieved of her bags and jewellery. At 3.00am she knocked on our door. She had been twice around the island road that loops past where we were, she had knocked on the doors of several villas asking for Janny. Her luggage was intact, she was intact; both were delivered by a bemused taxi driver who lugged her suitcases up the stairs after her.

'Janny,' she said, 'I don't know how on earth I got lost. I gave him your directions.' I imagined her leaning forward over the back of his seat, her voice rising and her vowels flattening in her efforts to help him to understand. Her speech was breathless, her eyes sparkled. It took a couple of hours and a glass of brandy to bring her down to a state where she could sleep.

Her travel misadventures in Europe thus far had been inadvertent, potentially dangerous, and typical consequences of that part of her personality that randomly bucked the system. In Paris she and her fellow silver-haired travellers had been taken to Montmartre and let loose to explore, with admonitions to be back at the bus by 7.00pm. Sylvia was not there at seven, and was still not back at the bus at 8.00pm. The bus driver closed the bus doors – what else could he do? He had a gaggle of tired and irritable pensioners on board. He took his impatient seniors back to the hotel, leaving my mother to find her own way. No-one knows and she can't remember how she found the hotel on the other side of Paris, wandering vaguely on the boulevards with her handbag a beacon for the eyes of snatchers.

The next morning in Crete, she appeared in the kitchen of the Cristi apartment complaining that there was no bath. Showers were not in her repertoire. She was dressed as she would be for a visit to a city, lipstick applied for the day. She was ready to be entertained. That afternoon, in thirty degrees she sat on the beach, tights on under her dress and a hat pulled down onto her hair under an umbrella we had hired for her. Her lips pursed a little when I swam topless like all the other women in their twenties and thirties. She said nothing on the beach. Later:

'Janny, do you think it is good for your baby, you swimming like that?'

'Like what, Mum?'

'Well, you know, naked, dear.'

I didn't attempt to unravel her logic.

A few days later we went with her by bus to the airport and escorted her to the plane that was taking her back to New Zealand first class, in the protection of airline staff who spoke the same language with the same accent, and were paid to understand her needs.

* * *

Morning sickness held hands with the low-grade fear that made runnels in my body, my thoughts and my sleep. The nausea was unremitting.

I found myself longing to be back in Christchurch, though it was driven by a desire for the time of nausea to pass. I consumed a constant trickle of food – especially eggs, potato and nuts, so that by the end of each day I was stuffed and uncomfortable.

Two weeks in Crete seemed too long. It felt like a marking of time before action. I wasn't sure, though, what that action was – perhaps it was going home? I knew I should be feeling relaxed, timeless, in the present. At one level that was how I usually felt, a level that was not hard to maintain except at unguarded moments such as just waking up. It was perhaps the dull, unremitting nausea –always a bitter-sweet acidity in the mouth, an unease in the stomach, a sense of unreality from, and inertia toward, what was happening around me. To be in New Zealand was also to be two weeks further toward the end of the pregnancy. It was impossible to think of the constant nausea and fear as contributing to a live baby – it was merely a happening somewhere near my pelvic girdle, at times a dark source of misery.

We ate at nearby tavernas. In our wanderings during the day we would choose one and go in to meet the owners. They took us out to their kitchens: small hot sheds with sloping roofs, where open pots simmered. Different hues of brown, odours mingling and inseparable. The chef would wave his hand in the direction of a pot, tell us what was in it, suggest that it was the best we would ever taste. A second and third pot would be similarly recommended. We made our decisions rapidly, needing to get out of the over-heated space. By the evening we had forgotten what we had chosen; whatever came was unfailingly delicious, and we could not tell whether or not it was what we had selected that morning.

The Greeks understood pregnancy; as soon they found out that I was having a baby, bowls of yoghurt with honey pooled on top were brought to the table.

'You should eat this, for your baby, for you.' They and the food were ambrosia for my sickly stomach and queasy soul.

A few days later Barbara and Iain, two-year-old Anna and baby Jonathan joined us at the Cristi apartments. Each day we visited new tavernas where we were welcomed by the unshaven chefs who by now knew Jim and me and our two *teknon*. Eight of us, happy families with a hole in the middle that would be filled by what for now was a dot in my vexatious tummy.

Barbara and I decided one morning that instead of going out to eat we would cook an evening meal in the apartment. It had a stove of sorts, and we had seen a butcher's shop in Hersonissou. The shop was an open shed with a chopping block outside, and there was undisguised evidence of meat cleavage on the ground around it. Through the eyes of carnivores, it was a happy sight; for vegetarians it would have provided gory justification for their eschewing meat. Barbara and I took the morning bus to the village, and returned triumphant with a bag of steak – enough to feed our red-blooded men and our energetic children.

In the early evening we took some pieces out to cook for the children. It slipped from the bag, fresh and bright red.

'Barb, look at the colour of this meat. Where do you think it comes from?'

She lowered her face close to the steaks.

'Cows? But, I can't remember seeing any cows on the island.'

'Neither have I. Have you ever eaten horse meat? I had some in Cambridge once, it looked just like this.'

Barbara tasted the meat we were frying for the children. Horse, or perhaps donkey; definitely not beef or lamb. The children ate like hungry puppies. After they had gone to bed we served it to Jim and Iain, who ate it with as much pleasure as the children and without comment. When the meal was finished we pointed out to them the absence of cows and sheep on the island. They had not noticed but they were happy. I pushed mine around my plate, not because I felt squeamish about its source, but from my evening morning sickness.

It doesn't make sense, that term, for the twenty-four-hour nausea of pregnancy.

Twenty-Four

It was October, late spring in Christchurch. We re-inhabited our home, our rangy two-storeyed house settled in its nest of English trees. The house was surrounded by trees in blossom. Its ceilings felt high and light, its arms curved around us and welcomed us. Simon and Emily went back to their school, their English accents evaporating in a blast of flat vowels and their memories of their forever friends in Bygrave dimming.

Our friends welcomed us, and stepped carefully around the subject of Alexander. Most had written to us in England telling us of their distress and love; now they were meeting us face-to-face with months between Alexander's death and the present. His life and death were events that had occurred twelve thousand miles away. They had no immediate connection to what had happened and no way of knowing how we would be. So meeting them again risked picking off the healing surfaces of our wounds while for them our responses and our emotional states were unpredictable. Some asked us directly – 'How are you?' or 'Tell us about Alexander, we are so sad that we did not meet him.' Others could not talk about him; they talked about our travels, how much Simon and Emily had grown, how their own children were doing. They left no gaps where the topic of a baby's death could arise. By now, though, we were a little stronger and a lot more understanding of the responses we met. It pricked, that avoidance, but it no longer punctured.

* * *

Inside me was a new life, a secret hopeful wonder, increasingly savoured for its own sake. For us it was a miracle that it existed – so easily it might not have been conceived. The randomness, the kindness of timing, meant that my new baby was growing. And by now it had transformed from an anonymous source of nausea to a small well of future happiness. I held its preciousness close.

It was time to have an amniocentesis. Then, that was the only way to test for Down Syndrome. Today, a blood test at twelve weeks' pregnancy tells the same story with only minor bodily invasion. I had had an amniocentesis when I was pregnant with Alexander, for the same reasons as I was having one now.

I was the wife of a doctor and therefore subject to increased collegial precaution. Doctors look after other doctors' families especially carefully; they fear living with a mistake that affects someone they know personally as well as in the surgery.

And now there were the added pressures of being a year older, and of being anxious in the certainty that things can go wrong

– although amniocentesis was not going to predict cot death. To have an amniocentesis felt like an inevitability rather than a considered decision.

I was lying on a bed in the obstetrician's clinic. I should have felt at ease, should not have flinched as the needle the length of his forearm loomed above my stomach. The last time it happened nothing had gone awry. But I didn't know this doctor. He was a rock star obstetrician, in his own estimation and in that of the Christchurch wives who clamoured to have him as their specialist. He was doing my amniocentesis because the elderly self-effacing obstetrician whom I did trust, and who was managing my pregnancy, was out of town. This man was appealing in the way that some professional people are, enhancing their physical attractiveness with an air of confidence, of swashbuckling, of slightly condescending assurance. He was personable in an I-know-what-I'm-doing sort of way. No problems, Jan! Risk? Almost none. Trust me. Just relax. He'd used ultrasound to locate my foetus; his confidence that his needle would miss it was not reassuring to me. Babies move, even sixteen-week foetuses. I wanted less talk, more focus.

The needle slid through the wall of my tummy into my uterus, and into the amniotic sac. It was painless but the sense of invasion was profound. The needle found a well of amniotic fluid, the doctor pulled its svelte shaft upwards and sucked it out of that private, sealed place where my baby was swimming. He pulled the needle out of my abdomen, waving it at me.

'Done! Easy, you see. Now, Jan, you go home and don't think about it for a month.'

I knew it was the right and sensible thing to have done. In a few weeks we would be reassured that this baby didn't have Down Syndrome. Or we would face a momentous decision. I had had enough of those in the last year. They call on wells of strength that were drained dry in me; I was surviving on surface water.

I was sixteen weeks' pregnant, well within the time zone when on a fourth pregnancy I should feel the baby's movements. There was nothing, no stirring inside. A week, two weeks later, there were no kicks or flutters, none of those enchanting tickling sensations that only women carrying babies can experience, that mark the first communications from the wriggling being inside.

Three weeks on, I was convinced that the baby had died. I was given an unscheduled ultrasound to reassure me that its heart was still beating, but I was the mother here. No movement; to my anxious self that meant no life.

Jim and I had not had a discussion about what we would do if the foetus was Down Syndrome. The implicit agreement between us was that if it was, I would have an abortion. Otherwise, why would we have had an amniocentesis? In those elongated four weeks between needle and results I made up my mind that I would not have this baby aborted if it was a Down baby. Down Syndrome was minor compared to the vegetative state I was prepared to contemplate had Alexander survived. The notion of dispensing with a baby deliberately simply because it was going to be different, where it would struggle in a world where cognitive ability was first prize, felt wrong. Compared with caring for someone whose functioning would have been utterly minimal had he lived, it was minor. I was as surprised at this decision as Jim was puzzled. I had always respected, and still do respect, the right of a woman to make decisions about her body. Jim was unhappy with my change of heart; I was sullen and determined. We waited.

The obstetrician's nurse phoned. 'Your baby is normal, Mrs Watt, no sign of Down's. And I'm sure you will be happy to know it is a girl.'

A normal baby, a girl baby. We did not have a preference for a boy, or for a girl. I had not wanted to know. Now I did, and now there was one characteristic by which she could not possibly be conflated with Alexander. Another line in the boundary between him and this baby was etched.

The next day this baby, this daughter, started dancing. Elbows and knees and head and bottom bounced and drummed on the wall of my abdomen – no butterfly flutters from her. She was fine, and my body was ready to receive her messages. I revelled in her exuberance, I relaxed into her existence, I looked forward to her birth.

Half way there. A healthy baby, no more sickness, the fogs were dispersing. The busyness of children and of being a wife in the suburbs of Christchurch expanded exponentially with the arrival of a puppy. Meg was a silver Great Dane, all limbs, a splayed velvet baby who arrived trembling in a crate at the airport and climbed onto Jim's knees every evening for two weeks until she outgrew even his long-legged lap. Her legs dangled over his knees and scraped the floor, her head flopped onto his forearm. She lay beside our old boxer, her expanding muzzle across the old girl's faded tummy, a ridiculous cuckoo of a puppy wanting to be mothered by a dog who was already smaller than her. She lolloped around the house, legs visibly longer each day, eating in proportion to the speed of her growth.

It was eight months after Alexander's death and it was Christmas. The house filled with Jim's parents and his brother's family from Auckland. Adults sat on the edge of the pool as child bodies leapt in and out, shining and fearless in the sun.

Grandparents, fathers and mothers watched, played, fed and adored. On Christmas day eleven bodies gathered around the dinner table. Christmas crackers were pulled, the jokes inside vied with daddy jokes for banality. Paper hats perched like birds on adult heads and fell around the ears of children. Grandparents submerged themselves in the warmth of children and grandchildren delighting in each other. Three generations were loving, laughing, overfilling on turkey and Christmas pudding, sleeping and sprawling in our sunbathed house.

My belly was swelling, curving outward through loose summer clothing. I was a serene Madonna, inwardly jittering at the edges of family joy.

* * *

In February 1982 I went back to the Psychology Department at the university and enrolled to do a doctorate.

'Are you sure you want to do this?' my supervisor asked. I was sure. I *needed* to do it. It was an outlet for the persistent hunger for intellectual activity, and it was a way of distracting myself from the tenacious hum of anxiety that took over whenever there was a lapse in my vigilance. It provided a channel to focus away from fearing for the baby I was carrying – or so I told myself.

I wanted to study babies – I knew that much. It might have been tempting to tackle the topic of SIDS, to look for an answer to the question of why Alexander and other babies had died. It could have been a tantalising possibility to attempt to solve the mystery.

I was not tempted. SIDS is not a psychological issue, it is a medical one, and I was in a Psychology faculty. And I had just enough insight to know that to spend three years or more focusing on a topic freighted for me with emotion would have been to border on an obsession with the subject. My experiences would have extinguished any chance of an objective enquiry.

Instead, encouraged by a paediatrician friend, I decided to focus on small-for-gestational-age and preterm infants in the first few months of their lives. I wanted to find out whether it helped them to flourish by having different kinds of parenting in those critical first days and weeks of their lives. And I wanted to know whether, as clinicians suspected, babies behaved differently if they were born small or early. For the next four months I sat with my distending tummy beside newborns in the neonatal ward and charted their breathing, their sleep states and their eye movements. Every ten seconds a buzzer beeped in my ear and I put a dash in the column that corresponded to their levels of breathing, what their eyes were doing, and what was happening at that moment as they slept. Their sleeping patterns would give a clue to the ways they organised the vital functions of their bodies. Later I would watch them with their mothers to see how they were being handled. I would assess their development, and see if there were links between their mothers' behaviour and their progress. If so, it might be possible to teach mothers how best to respond to their tiny or preterm infants.

All very worthy, all very objective, and I published several academic papers reporting my findings. It is only looking back that I see the significance of the compulsion to be near small, breathing, alive babies. Meantime, the baby that was tossing around in my insides seemed removed from all of this, a life of her own with no relevance to what I was doing. Instead of listening to her and focusing on her squirms, I was watching over other people's babies.

Twenty-Five

April 1982. The city of Christchurch strutted its finest in these months, paraded its English roots. Cool mornings presaged the winter to come. The light flowed low across the roads, through the parks, filtered through the tints of autumn leaves. Maples and claret ash glowed red, gleditsia and gingko shone yellow, oaks and ashes straddled the palate from lemon to darkest bronze. There was the calmness of a summer both spent and well-spent, and a winter sleepiness to come, bridged by the serene dissipation of autumn. According to the calculations of the obstetrician, my baby was due to be born just a year after Alexander had died.

My parents-in-law had arrived poised to take care of Simon and Emily. They settled into the spare bedroom, took command of the kitchen, and readied themselves for grandchild care. Nothing happened. A week passed. Ligaments stretched, threatened to let go of the burden that was overwhelming them in this fourth pregnancy. Still no labour, still no baby. I sat around the house, a bumpy mass of discomfort.

Why was she waiting? I wanted her in my arms, I wanted her safely out of my body, I wanted to meet her and to welcome her to her family. Perhaps she was scared to emerge. Maybe she was too comfortable in her warm and cramped bath. And then I remembered Emily. Her reluctance to be born had led to medical intervention – it just happens with some babies. I relaxed, stepped away from irrational worries.

But she, too, exceeded the limits of obstetric tolerance. At the end of the second week my obstetrician decided to get her out. This time I was ready, this time birth would be dignified, this time I would be in control. I had done this three times before, I knew what to expect. A beanbag was waiting for me in the delivery suite as the oxytocin started to urge my body into action in the labour ward.

And this time my body would not wait - I did not make it to the beanbag. I called time in the labour ward and a rush of orderlies appeared and wheeled the bed out through the swing doors to take me through to the delivery suite. This daughter did not linger. She arrived between my legs on the trolley in the corridor on the way.

She lay on the trolley sheet, still attached to me. She was pink and purple and calm, and she was perfect. She was lifted, covered in the white vernix that had protected her skin in utero, onto my chest and into my arms. Someone dressed in white dealt with the umbilical cord as I held her. Dark eyes and, I imagined, a knowingness and wisdom. I was oblivious to the fussing of the medical staff who were trying to help me to expel the placenta. Someone tried to pry my baby from me while they dealt with the aftermath of a birth in the wrong part of the hospital. I resisted; they let her stay lying on my stomach.

I was in love with this baby immediately – ridiculously, passionately, happily adoring her messy newborn self. No doubt hormonal elation had something to do with it. I had been given oxytocin to go into labour; prolactin and beta-endorphins were surging through my body. It was so much more than hormones, though. She was the small, slippery red embodiment of our joy, the joy we deserved after the year of tumult and grief. I lay on the trolley and adored her.

An hour later I was lying in a bed in a ward. Outside was an autumn blackbird chorusing his delight in being alive; beside me was my daughter, newborn, asleep. She had scrubbed up well. Her hair was exuberantly black, her skin creamy, the shape of her chin displayed the gentle determination that has been her paramount asset all her life.

I knew her flawlessness was fragile. It was miraculous, and I stilled the quiet murmur reminding me that perfect babies can die. I had a rational voice, even then, that reminded me that our first two children survived and thrived. In their infancies sheepskins were their mattresses, their comfort, the material in which they buried their faces so sensuously. And they slept on their tummies. Child-rearing experts were quite clear in the 1970s that babies might have choked if they slept on their backs. And most of them did not die. I knew just enough in

1982, though, to decide that this baby would not sleep on a sheepskin, and she would sleep on her back.

We named her Esther. It was her paternal grandmother's name, though that was partly coincidental – we liked the name. My mother's name, Sylvia, was not in contention. It was deeply unfashionable in the Eighties. Sylvia did her best to conceal her disappointment when she arrived at the hospital to inspect her granddaughter.

'If she's going to be Esther from Jim's side, then her second name must be Jan, from our side.'

Churlishly, I failed to tell her that I was grateful for her restraint. And I failed to understand quite how she felt.

We went home to another big-boned house, this time in the southern hemisphere, to the arms of her father, brother and sister. We were again a tight five, a group that felt the right size, a number that worked for us.

Simon's and Emily's lives were inhabited with school, music, sport and friends. Jim was immersed in his medical practice. As it had been with Alexander, Esther and I were in this together. I could not leave her alone. She slept in a baby cocoon, I carried her from room to room, to the supermarket, to the bank.

Sometimes my anxiety erupted. I was in the post office at the university, in line waiting to be served. The others in the queue were students, twenty years younger than me. Some, it seemed, had not showered for several days; a whiff of stale armpits permeated the small room. At my feet was Esther, in the cocoon, asleep. I shuffled her along with my shoes as I moved up the line.

It was my turn at the counter. As the teller greeted me, I glanced down. Esther was pale, and utterly still. I could not see her breathing. Swamping with panic, I swooped down, snatched her from her bedding, and held her up. She was breathing, she was alive, and now she was awake and crying. I took her outside, ducking the stares of the students in the queue behind me, and reassembled the bedding and the baby. I decided not to go back and get the stamps.

In 1982, breathing monitors were both crude and uncommon. Jim's paediatrician brother Mike sent us one from Auckland Hospital, where he worked. It was a clunky machine, fired by batteries and with a dial that could be set to a length of time after which it would beep if it detected no breathing. We took it out of the box labelled 'bandages', held it up. It had a cord hanging from the dial, a yellowing worm attached to a coin-shaped sensor at the other end. We cut long swathes of sticky tape and we taped the sensor to Esther's tummy. It was a conspicuous emblem of our anxieties, stuck on to delicate baby skin. It was an invasion and a relief.

The machine clicked with every breath, with every minute rise and fall of her tummy, a constant reassurance that she was still breathing. I became addicted to the clicking, the measure of her living. It counted her breaths, it soothed the panic that lurked under my surface calm, waiting to burst through. Sometimes it went off – perhaps it missed a tiny breath, perhaps she did stop breathing for the thirty seconds it was set to wait before bleeping the alarm. Jim or I raced to her cot, to find her alive and asleep. Fear is exhausting. I was like a rag doll for a few minutes after each dash to save her.

The monitor was an unsophisticated device, its false alarms wearying. I was grateful for its clumsy presence.

* * *

Early September. A blackbird sang his song of spring, of optimism, in the puriri tree in the front garden. The sun had moved up in the sky from its winter trajectory across the line of the rooftops to the north, made its way through the window glass and warmed the jasmine tumbling out of the terracotta pot in the conservatory. Lemon streaks of sun crossed the conservatory floor and flowed into the bedroom opening onto it. The extravagant perfume of the jasmine bled through the house. The feeling of air on my bare arms was buoying.

Esther lay on the bed, the sun highlighting glances of auburn in the black mass of her hair. She was giggling, the deep chortle that consumes baby bodies, taking them over and infecting anyone who hears. She was naked in the spring warmth, naked except for the tape holding the breathing monitor on the skin of her tummy. It had been there, a crooked cross, for five months.

It was time to take it off.

I lifted the edge of the tape that criss-crossed her body. It yielded, peeled away from her baby skin, leaving blushes of pink where it had held my panics and fears at bay for twenty weeks. I pared it away, each millimetre releasing my daughter a little more from her mother's anxieties.

She lay bare, freed from the bindings that were the legacy of Alexander's death. She was just Esther, entirely Esther, her own life-embracing self. She banged her heels on the bed, legs and arms waving like mini windmills. And I knew we had come through. I knew we would be just fine.

Twenty-Six

The nightingale has a lyre of gold,
The lark's is a clarion call,
And the blackbird plays but a boxwood flute,
But I love him best of all.

For his song is all of the joy of life,
And we in the mad, spring weather,
We two have listened till he sang
Our hearts and lips together.

Frederick Tennyson

It is still challenging when a person who does not know about Alexander recoils at the news of his existence and death. I remind myself that their reaction is normal, that it embodies sympathy alongside embarrassment and helplessness. But the desire to acknowledge and honour his life is still intact. A major reason for writing this book is to try to combat that pulling-back, that withdrawal from something real and central to who I am. It is to encourage acknowledgement of dead babies and children.

In the first years after Alexander died, the sound of an ambulance wailing its way to a call-out felled me. The horror and helplessness flooded back, visceral responses to that Friday when we drove, the ambulance screaming for passage through the morass of A1 London-bound traffic. Sirens no longer slice through my heart.

I still want to protect other people's babies. I was sitting at the dinner table five years ago with English friends of friends who were living in New Zealand for a year. As we were starting the meal, I was aware of their three-and-a-half-month-old baby who was sick in the next room. He was silent. They were relieved that he was not crying. I longed for him to cry, to let us know that he was still alive. The urge to go and check on him was only just usurped by good manners; I hardly knew these parents, and they were doctors. I assured myself that they knew how to look after their infant.

* * *

Twice a year, on 20th December, his birthday, and 10th April – the date when he died - I burn a candle for Alexander. A Jewish friend gave me a yahrzeit candle that illuminated these times of remembering for several years. 'Yahrzeit' is a memorial, or soul candle.

Once I lit a candle for Alexander in Notre-Dame. A secular act in a place of worship; it felt appropriate to do it as a symbolic, not a religious, act. There is something about candles – serenity, peace, quietness, light, warmth, tenderness.

This year, I drank a glass of red wine in a strange pub in London.

On two occasions since his death, grief has overtaken me without warning. In 1992, eleven years after he died, I was teaching a group of graduate students. The subject was SIDS. Twelve clever and ambitious young people fidgeted as I set up the video machine in a stifling room in the Auckland Medical School. Blinds were drawn against the sun across the open windows. As the video started, I began to drown. Sorrow surged up past my heart and through my throat. My body gave me no warning, no signal that grief still lurked under the surface. My confidence that I could address the topic objectively was in tatters. I fled the room silently, left the students to watch by themselves.

A year later I was in a neonatal intensive care ward in Brisbane, Australia. I was one of a miscellany of researchers and paediatricians doing a ward round. We stopped at the bedside of each scrap of human being lying silent and sick, tubes in and tubes out of minuscule veins and throats. As the entourage drew to a halt at each cot or incubator, the consultant murmured information to the ten of us gathered around. The details of each small patient were discussed, questions passed back and forth amongst intelligent, compassionate, and often puzzled professionals. Beside the bed of a seemingly healthy dark-haired baby who was dying without any reason the doctors could discern, the world went black. My legs sagged and I slumped to the floor like a helium balloon losing its gas. Someone put me in the recovery position, and consciousness seeped back. I re-joined the caravan of white coats, lurked at the edges of the group, and twice more during the round flopped to the floor. No-one asked why I was fainting – an odd lack of reaction from medical professionals. I was surprised, and relieved. I could not have found words to explain.

Sorrow persists, even as it loses its vigour. Now, years after those startling experiences, it no longer creeps up to assault me from behind. It has diluted to an easy sadness, a reassurance that Alexander's memory is alive.

* * *

Co-dependence is a word with a whiff of shame. It invokes images of alcohol and drugs, of two people yoked helplessly under the influence of something powerful and negative. In 1999 I was at a Human Development Conference in Sydney. A clutch of researchers and their graduate students had gathered for three days at a university that, like most, took advantage of academic breaks by hosting conferences and topping up their coffers.

As well as the smorgasbord of scholarly oral presentations there was the accompanying display of posters. Posters are the venue for displaying the findings of Ph.D students, and sometimes of fledged academics who would rather construct a visual account of their work than prepare an oral presentation.

I slipped out the side door from an oral session on adolescent attachment and drifted into the hall of posters. There were rows of carefully created displays, each one with its unburnished Ph.D student in attendance, corridors of the academically hopeful. My eyes skimmed elaborate models with beta weights and significant pathways looking like the wires on the electronics of a computer and signalling the gravity of the findings. I read solemn conclusions about what these depictions of human behaviour might mean, I looked at earnest suggestions for future research. These were brave, optimistic, and sometimes remarkably naïve stories based on hours of statistical or qualitative analyses; they were the stuff of future research careers.

A forty-font title stopped my trajectory down the aisle. Three words blazed out from the rest. "Cot Death" and "Co-dependence". A young woman beside the poster smiled invitingly, like the owner of a shop where I was the only customer to have entered the doors that day. She invited me to read her display. Her hypothesis was that the relationship between a parent – especially a mother – and a child born after its sibling's death through SIDS, is likely to be one of co-dependence.

Co-dependence is a diffuse notion. Its salient characteristics in such a situation are likely to be a compulsive mutual need for each other, and fear of being apart or being alone. Were Esther and I co-dependent? This was not an academic question for me. Had I smothered her individuality? Had I prevented her from growing into her own independent self? Had I rendered her dependent on my presence and attention?

As I stood listening to the student's narrative in Australia, Esther was in England. She was seventeen. She was on a gap year tutoring English girls at a school in Bristol, some of whom were older than her. She was also working under-age in a pub as a bar woman in the evenings, and was about to travel around Europe out of contact with me, with friends for three weeks. That did not seem to accord with a notion of co-dependency. I missed her, but no more or less than I missed Emily in Wellington and Simon in London.

I think we escaped unhealthy mutual neediness. We were not co-dependent.

Twenty-Seven

Men and women tend to grieve in different ways. Typically, men in western societies do not display their grief and rage. Subtle and not-so-restrained pressures are on them from birth not to cry - to be strong, to carry on. And because this is their mode of behaviour, others assume that they are all right, that they will not welcome hugs or acknowledgement of their pain. It works in tandem – men's behaviour and people's assumptions join to reinforce their apparent stoicism.

I had no understanding about how Jim was feeling in the months after Alexander died. As we sat with him when he was dying we held each other, cried together, hoped together. We tag-teamed sitting with him when the other needed a shower or a break. When he died, like two linked automatons we planned the funeral together.

We wrapped our children in our arms, reassured and hugged them, listened to their distress and confusion and tried to hold them through their grief. In the weeks and months after Alexander died we focused laser-like on Simon and Emily, and we were unaware of the susceptibility of our relationship to erosion. The superficial layers of living demanded attention and resources, depleting our reserves so that nothing was left for the real work that needed to be done, wrapping each other in our arms, taking the emotionally hard path of pulling together. We thought we were strong, strong enough to get through this intact as a couple, as parents. As far as we knew there were no chinks, no vulnerabilities in our relationship.

I thought then that we were supporting each other. In July 1981 I wrote in my diary:

Strangely Alexander's death has left some residues of increased strength. Jim's and my relationship may not fare well through navigating experiences on the continent, but it has not just survived but been reinforced by the sharing of this grief.

Others, too, thought we were strong. The doctors and nurses at Great Ormond Street Hospital remarked on how well we had managed Alexander's dying and death. What does "well" mean? We did not collapse, physically or emotionally, by the side of his cot. Perhaps we seemed calm and accepting of whatever might happen. We were, though, screaming and pleading inside.

Yet, looking back, there were signs of distress. Later in July 1981 I noted in my diary: *Jim withdrew from us all and I reacted negatively.*

And: *We don't spend enough time just being together for each other.*

Also: *It becomes very draining, I find, trying to support both (my mother) and Jim, whose needs sometimes conflict.*

My diary at that time chronicles a life of hectic activity in those months between Alexander's death and leaving the UK for New Zealand. Jim was working long hours at the medical centre, while I ran the children and myself to exhaustion visiting friends, going to London – drowning, at least in part, the hum of grief. And as we prepared to leave, neighbours and friends beyond the village sought last chances to see us. We spent most weekends travelling to Cornwall, to London, to Cambridge, to farewell families we had come to know well. No time to stop, no time to reflect.

We did not seek advice and support outside our family, and no-one offered it. We blundered on doing what we thought was of overriding importance – being sensitive to Simon and Emily. We forgot, though, to check in with each other. We made assumptions about the other's wellbeing, day to day. At the end of a workday when Jim needed quiet and time to grieve, I fell on him demanding his support. I had been alone all day, and I was too soggy and self-absorbed to be his rock. I was time-rich and lonely; Jim was working every day with no time to feel. At first I ladled my distress on to Barbara's pregnant self. She was an anchor as I raged and wept. Her ability to simply cry with me rather than searching for well-meaning words was exactly right. She guided my navigation through those sorrow-soaked days. Yet she was having her own baby. I realised only fleetingly how onerous my demands for comfort must have been.

Looking back, I see myself swamped in my own grief, focusing only on the children and on getting myself out of bed every day. Almost as rote, I would ask Jim how he was feeling at the end of the day. Perhaps I did not hear his sadness, his despair. He seemed strong, he seemed okay.

I do not know where Jim found his solace. Maybe he found none.

It felt then, and it feels now, as if there were no scripts to get us through and to help us emerge intact as a couple. We had no knowledge about how to help each other mourn. We did not see that we were embarking on different trajectories. An impermeable screen grew up between us that was imperceptible in the busyness of our lives.

The drift continued, unacknowledged, as we settled back into our life in New Zealand with Esther. Jim worked hard, very hard, paying our mortgage and tending to the needs of his patients. They took all his emotional energy, leaving little for the family. One of his patients, a schoolmaster's wife in Christchurch, gushed to me once that he'd held her head while she vomited when she was pregnant. I was gutted. He rarely comforted me when I was sick. And yet I was one who suffered silently, suppressing pain and the need for comfort to a ridiculous extent. I was *too* stoic, reacting against my mother's hypochondriasis. How could Jim support me when I refused to acknowledge that I needed it?

I felt unloved; I was unlovable. I was propelled by an unhealthy compulsion to get A grades for my graduate papers. Maybe my stores of passion did not stretch to mothering, studies, *and* my relationship.

I tried. One day I called Jim's medical centre.

'Could I make an appointment to see Jim, please?' Startled, the receptionist gave me a time. I needed to have his attention – a whole fifteen minutes for which I would willingly have paid. I told her not to do it – I was fine, really I was.

'Can we please talk about our relationship?' I would ask.

'I'm tired,' he would say. 'You can talk but I'm probably too exhausted to listen.'

And he was.

I suggested we get some counselling for our communication troubles. That was confrontational for a person whose work encompassed counselling others. He was both able and sympathetic as a counsellor. It was too difficult for him to agree. I understand that now; I did not then.

I know now that the loss of a baby or a child can spear the heart of a marriage. The loss can evoke the poisons of blame and recrimination; it finds vulnerabilities and expands them. It can fire each person off on a separate trajectory of mourning until they lose sight of each other and of the things that held them close.

Many marriages survive this kind of tragedy. Ours fell apart, six years after Alexander's death. We blamed anything but his loss. We found faults in each other, we fell "out of love", too late we sought help in counselling. We went our separate but closely linked ways.

Only occasionally did I wonder if Alexander's death had contributed. Now I see the unfolding trajectory of pain, of neglect of each other's needs, of both of us immersing in the distraction of work. Yet we thought we were surviving as a couple. Maybe, just maybe, if someone had told us at the time that we would react in different ways to losing him, that we needed to focus on each other in order to support our children, our marriage might have survived.

Most of all when I think of how Alexander fits into the past I think of you and Dad. And how devastating and awful and sad it was for you both. The only way to come close to understanding is to think about how it would affect me if I lost one of our kids... I think one reason I have no rancour about you and Dad divorcing is the comprehension that almost no marriage can survive the loss of a baby   Simon, 2014

Today, Jim is happily together with another person, a woman who complements him perfectly. He and I have parented Simon and Emily and Esther shoulder-to-shoulder since we separated. Their sporadic attempts to divide and conquer when they were teenagers failed. They have three adults who care unconditionally for them.

Twenty-Eight

We are grandparents. We have relationships with our children that are elaborated and enriched as they themselves have become parents. They are wise, so much wiser than I was as a parent. Their love for their babies is primal and tender.

I am in thrall to being a grandparent. Like giving birth, it is an experience that no-one can explain, a privilege that verges on universal at the same time as being utterly unique. It is a role that spans the gamut from no involvement to full-time parenting.

These babies of our babies deserve the absolute best we can be for them. Their warm, wriggling, present bodies, and the frightening world we are leaving for them, demand that we grandparent as well as we can.

In my head I have an ideal, a paradigm for grandmothering. I want to be a calm, wise and loving figure who is there as a not-mother, as neither a mother-alternative nor mother-competitor. I want to be grounded and in a state of grace toward my grandchildren. I want to be a resource, unconditional and ever-accessible to the generation being spawned by my children.

I have, though, no idea how to be this grandmother. Being calm, wise and in a state of grace is a continuous hope, an aspiration that I may never attain. I have few scripts to follow, and they are hard to read. The one grandmother alive in my childhood was my mother's mother, a woman diluted into blandness, who played no memorable part in my life. She was not a source of comfort, nor of inspiration or strength, nor even a model of personhood against whom I could rail. She was a pale, insubstantial woman in all ways, memories of whom are dominated by her stock phrase – 'That's nice, dear.' It was her response to everything, happy or sad. She cooked me brains for lunch when I was a child. She was at the edge of our lives, living in the small house behind ours that my father built for my grandfather and her.

My paternal grandmother, Emily Jane, is a photograph. Her face is level, symmetrical, her eyes steady and her jawline strong. Her gaze shines out of the picture, surmounting the encumbrance of the dress and bonnet that was the fashion of the day. She had five children, just one of whom was a daughter. Her husband beside her in the photo has an oval, bearded, and - compared with hers - weak face. He died young, and she raised her sons and daughter in the poverty of small-town widowhood. I wish I had known her. She just might have been strong and wise, loving and inspirational. She might have been what my maternal grandmother was not. She might, too, have been stern and forthright and cool. Her photo suggests that at least she would have been a presence.

My mother grandmothered my children mainly in the sense of being a legal and biological noun. She was absorbed by herself, her anger, and her insecurities. She needed my children to love her. She bribed Simon with secret handouts of money. She criticised Emily and her friends in front of them. At the dinner table one night when Emily, aged eight, had a shy friend to stay:

'Emily, doesn't your little friend like us? She doesn't *say* anything.'

My children built their defences young, indulged her neediness and loved her dutifully. She had a notion of the role a grandparent should play that involved giving things, especially money, and being seen to be loved by them. She was incapable of being involved in that primeval way that knots you to grandbabies.

In contrast, my mother-in-law grandmothered unconditionally. She was, as long as her body allowed, the perfect playmate. Her capacity to push swings, read books, play hide-and-seek and laugh uproariously was boundless and extended across four households of grandchildren. She was of the kindest of her generation – self-denying, generous, and loving. She was the sweet, unchiding, all-accepting, grateful model of grandmothering. She is the best model I have.

Grandmothering, this role that has gripped my heart with fingers that don't let go, is accompanied by vulnerability to pain. The loss of a grandchild would be as devastating as the death of Alexander. Now I wonder how it was for Alexander's grandparents.

His paternal grandparents experienced a tragedy of timing, arriving in London two days after he died, grieving a baby they never met. They were there to hold us, to farewell him, to join the pool of sorrow. They set aside their loss of an unmet grandchild in the interests of supporting his parents. I don't know whether anyone acknowledged their particular and specific grief.

My mother, Sylvia, had her own idiosyncratic grief. She denied to herself that he might die; when he did she languished in New Zealand, writing letters of sadness and support. Her experience of loss was abundant, and existed alongside her ambivalence about his life and death. Had she thought about it, the juxtaposition would have been awkward.

The heartache of grandparents is often overlooked as the suffering of parents takes the primary focus when a child is lost. Parents lose children and grandparents lose grandchildren through miscarriage, through stillbirth and adoption and SIDS. The rope that binds grandparents to grandchildren can be heavy-duty; far too often it is severed without acknowledgement.

Our grandbabies are the ongoing threads of intergenerational connection, the legacy of whatever our lives may mean. We need these cords of hope and renewal as have grandparents before us. Through us, they just might come to know not only whatever shreds of wisdom we gleaned in our early baby-boomer lives, but especially what it means to belong - to belong to *this* family, *this* line of strong women and men, *this* woven thread of history, happiness, sadness and accumulated wisdom.

The intergenerational threads weave a fabric that feels inviolable. I know that it is not. Not one of my relationships is indestructible – Alexander taught me that. And so these relationships with grown-up children and grandchildren are celebrated, enjoyed, and cherished by the day. Somehow their colours are more vivid, their songs sweeter, because of that vulnerability.

I do not think this is strange. I do not think it is just a consequence of losing Alexander, a persisting reaction to my baby dying. I do think it is the heightened awareness of the preciousness of their lives, the day-to-day appreciation of them now, the knowledge that nothing is forever. Time renders the odds of seeing them reach adulthood as stacked against us; there is a poignancy and awareness of the fragility of the bond.

Only now can I comprehend the pain that grandparents are able to experience. No grandparent prepared me for the primal connection I feel to those babies of my babies. It is a rope of wire, of silk, of steel, of tenderness, of fierce, protective love. Some say it is a parent's role to lay down their life for their children. I am there beside them, ready to fight to the death for the survival of my grandchildren. The connection is intense, and as differently strong as it is to my own babies. They are my children's children. They are not mine, yet I feel a kind of non-possessive ownership that is perhaps no more than the rattling of the DNA chain that links us.

* * *

It was November 2013. I was looking after three-month-old Eliza for the evening. Her parents had gone out the door to have a meal together at a restaurant, their first date since she was born. They farewelled her fulsomely, they went into her bedroom three times to say goodbye to her. They were tired, excited and beautiful as they left. I imagined them looking at each other through veils of exhaustion, seeing each other again, restoring their energies.

I love this grandchild with a passion that is ferocious, the passion of a grandmother.

On this midweek evening while my granddaughter's parents were treasuring their few hours together, there was an extra frisson. Most babies today have their lives monitored. The monitors are not crude instruments strapped to their tummies as Esther's was. They are sensitive pieces of electronics that register via a mattress a baby's most minute movements. Beside me as I read in a chair was a blue object, like a large, unfashionable cell phone, that told me the temperature in her room. It had a swinging pendulum showing her inhalations and exhalations and, I knew, would scream an emergency should she stop inhaling and exhaling. I should have trusted it, but I didn't, quite.

I went to the door of her bedroom, pushed it just open, slid my body sideways into the gloom. She was on her back, in her sleeping suit. Her contours came into focus as my eyes adjusted. I could see the rise and fall of her chest.

I forgave myself this lack of faith in technology, this moment of irrationality.

Twenty-Nine

I know noble accents
And lucid, inescapable rhythms;
But I know, too,
That the blackbird is involved in what I know.
> *Sunday Morning* Stanza VIII, Wallace Stevens

Throughout Alexander's life, blackbirds sang. They sang when he was born, when he died, and they sang when Esther was born. They sing in England, they sing in New Zealand. Blackbirds are optimism, hopefulness and joy as they sing slightly off-key, and without guile. They sing as Alexander sang. And blackbirds are dark.

If I was to write a letter to myself, or to another mother, about what I have learned, it would go something like this:

You know, with deepest poignancy, the preciousness of babies. Your heart will blanch and curl at its edges when you see a baby neglected, ignored, seemingly unloved. You know that maybe that mother in the supermarket is depressed. Or she has no money. Or her partner beats her. And you suspect that she *wants* to love her baby. And you want to take her shoulders, shake them gently, and say 'please, love your baby.' You know they are precious, because yours died.

We must not take our children for granted.

And when your baby died, you were comforted. You knew your comforters loved you. You knew they wanted to staunch your hurt. And you found that what they were attempting to do was impossible.

Now you know what worked. They hugged you, hard. They talked about your son – how beautiful he was, how much you loved him, how much he loved you.

And you know what hurt. The exquisitely painful blows of denial, avoidance, stories to top yours, advice to get over it and to try again.

You know that you will not get over it. And you don't want to. Your baby is a part of you, of your past, present, and future. You know the joy he brought you. You would not have forsaken that in order to avoid the pain of losing him.

And so you know you are blessed, despite that pain. You had him to love. It hurts through the marrow of your heart that he has gone. It will forever.

And you are strong, resilient as the branch of a willow bent to the ground in the storm, rising back up to the sky tested and flourishing. You have grown in ways unimagined until now. You have survived the unthinkable – what powerful knowledge that is.

The world has changed forever; you are no longer guileless, optimistic, confident that it is a benign place. It is not, and you live with that truth more fully than before.

At the same time, you see those simple ciphers of perfection in your world in ways you did not before. They glow, they are flawless, they are not forever.

You have changed. You are not invincible, you are not a worker of miracles. You are so much more attuned with your self. You have faced your failings and mistakes, your fortitude and your grace. You are not better, you are not worse, you are so much more real.

* * *

The enigma at the heart of this story is the timing of Alexander's death, and the fact that it enabled Esther's life. It is the birth and life of a remarkable daughter who was so nearly not conceived and born. It is a conundrum that for me just exists. It needs no explanation. It simply happened, a quirk of time.

Es is such a huge part of our lives, and a wonderful vibrant person... and so the counterfactual of Alexander living and her never coming into existence is almost impossible to imagine... but I never dwell on this aspect really, it's too unreal and the reality of Es is so unequivocably fantastic. Simon, 2014

She is not a replacement Alexander. Instead, she occupies a space that is uniquely hers, Esther-shaped, that exists beside the existence of a place that Alexander can inhabit in our memories. We can exult in her, and delight in the brief time we had with him. It feels like a double blessing.

Carol, my friend in Scotland whom I never met, also had another child:

For the joy of another baby, for all the family, for the help in getting things into perspective – for myself, and also in allowing the appreciation of the short life of a child to be a positive one and one less encumbered by the sadness of this death; and for understanding the fact that some things like love remain while time's passing does ease pain – for all these reasons I'm so glad we took the plunge. The costs have been repaid more times than can be counted. Carol

Carol and I were lucky. We had the choice to have another baby. We might have decided not to face down the dilemmas involved. We knew what was at stake – the possibility that we would lose another child. It had happened, why risk it happening again?

Some parents choose not to have another baby, others cannot. If Jim and I had made that choice, if Alexander had died a week later than he did so that we had no choice, this story would nonetheless be one of optimism and triumph.

Epilogue

North London, April 2014. In my arms lies a baby boy. His hair is a raven halo around his face, the colour of a blackbird. His skin is clear, creamy, it smells milky-sweet. I can hear the passing of his breath in and out through his nose, the calm, even sound of living. His eyes are closed. I can see the blue-grey veins forming spider webs across the skin of his lids, which are quivering as he starts to dream. His mouth moves in a sketch of sucking; he has just finished filling his tummy with milk. He is replete and relaxed. His body softens into mine, his head slumps into the corner of my elbow and his body fits into the bumps and hollows of my lap.

I am holding, watching, listening, feeling, absorbing and adoring my grandson Finlay. He looks like Alexander, he is not Alexander. It is thirty-four years later.

It is a London spring day. Outside, the sun is pouring onto the garden, the footpaths, the treetops. I am the most blessed woman in the world. The blackbird on the chimney is singing his out-of-tune, life-affirming song.

Acknowledgements

A writer is a writer only when she or he is writing. And although she might imagine she is doing this alone, it would not happen without the generosity and understanding of others.

First, heartfelt thanks to my family who have shown selfless understanding and tolerance. Jim, Simon, Emily, Esther, Barbara and Iain, thank you for trusting me to write this. You have been unfailingly supportive.

Special thanks to Rae, Peter and Sue, who have provided unstinting support and encouragement.

I want to thank Carol, whose letters sustained me throughout the loss of Alexander. I count Carol as a special friend, one whom I have not yet met.

Thank you Rhonda, Julian, Suzanne, Ian, Linda, Janine, and Elinor; friends who have given me feedback and have never faltered in believing in the book.

To the family of 'Geordie', thank you for being happy with my account of his funeral.

To Martin, who features in this book, thank you for checking some facts and not minding how I describe you!

Thanks to Mark McCrum who inspired me to write and has offered constant encouragement throughout.

Warmest thanks to my editor, Katharine. You have done an amazing job and been a pleasure to work with.

This is my story, and so it is a singular perspective. Other stories of the same material may vary. I take full responsibility for what I have written, and I know that the stories of others may be different.

Permissions

It has been a pleasure to include the work of other authors, poets and academics throughout this book, with thanks for the following:

R.S. Thomas poem by generous permission of the Thomas family.

Collected Poems of Wallace Stevens: permission from Faber and Faber.

Excerpt from Christopher Reid: permission from Rogers, Coleridge and White Ltd.

Quote from *Levels of Life* (Julian Barnes): permission from Random House.

Quote from *Memorio of Mary Wilder White* courtesy of Elinor Horner.

www.ingramcontent.com/pod-product-compliance
Lightning Source LLC
Chambersburg PA
CBHW060518080526
44586CB00012B/528